I hope you are
inspired by this
book

from Majendi

MARLEY'S MEMOIR:

The Journey to an Irreversible Action and the Aftermath

MAJENDI JARRETT

WESTBOW
PRESS®

A DIVISION OF THOMAS NELSON
& ZONDERVAN

This book is a work of non-fiction. Unless otherwise noted, the author
and the publisher make no explicit guarantees as to the accuracy of
the information contained in this book and in some cases, names of
people and places have been altered to protect their privacy.

WestBow Press books may be ordered through booksellers or by contacting:

WestBow Press
A Division of Thomas Nelson & Zondervan
1663 Liberty Drive
Bloomington, IN 47403
www.westbowpress.com
844-714-3454

Scripture taken from the Amplified Bible, Copyright © 1954, 1958, 1962,
1964, 1965, 1987 by The Lockman Foundation. Used with permission.

ISBN: 978-1-6642-6871-5 (sc)
ISBN: 978-1-6642-6873-9 (hc)
ISBN: 978-1-6642-6872-2 (e)

Library of Congress Control Number: 2022910908

Print information available on the last page.

WestBow Press rev. date: 06/17/2022

Reflections from Friends

"A very hard read but well done. Great effort. Will inspire a lot of people."—H. Mitchell

"It is very honest and raw. I could not stop reading it until I finished." –J. Ansong

"It certainly makes compelling reading; you've done exceedingly well."—Z. Johnson

"It is a good account of Marley's life and I like the way you aligned your thoughts, so you get a complete picture of events."—J. Joyann

"A moving tale of teenage anguish and how a tragic event inspired a grieving family."—S. Lockyer

Marley Asher Adeshino Prescott
on the beach of Tokeh Village

Contents

PART II – THE AFTERMATH OF AN IRREVERSIBLE ACTION

Dedication

I dedicate this book to my son, Marley Asher Adeshino Prescott, I would rather have had the eighteen years with you than nothing at all and without you I would not have written this book.

Introduction

Since I was a little girl growing up, I loved reading. I loved writing essays and doing reading comprehension in school. I loved sharing about what I did on vacation or an interesting place I had visited.

This book started because I wanted to capture what was happening at the time. I wanted to document the weekly interactions with Marley, as at the time I thought this was teenage hormones that he would outgrow. I thought a good way of doing this was to write a book that I would give to Marley when he was older.

Although I always had a desire to write, this was not the book I had in mind. So, when I started this book, especially the chapters in Marley's voice, it wasn't intended for publication until the event that took place in December 2020. I realised others could benefit from what Marley experienced as he tried to navigate anxiety, social awkwardness, and depression. It took a lot of nudging from unlikely sources to take the first steps to finish the book. Then there was a lot of soul searching before I finally took the steps to complete the process of publishing the book.

Marley always sent me voicemail, as it was an easy way to express himself without interruption; sometimes it was how he felt, especially when there had been an argument and he had been unpleasant. Other times he used it to share his point of view on previous conversations in case he forgot, especially if I was away on business travel. He sent voicemails on WhatsApp or text messages, usually with an apology and to give some insight into how he was feeling.

After his demise, when I accessed his phone, I was able to see messages he had sent to online friends and also what he had captured in his mobile notepad. These and the many conversations we had over the years provided the material for his perspective in part two.

Watch out for *Living without Marley,* which is the sequel to *Marley's Memoir.*

Acknowledgements

I am grateful to my friends and family for supporting me and encouraging me to write this book. I thank God for everyone who has covered me in prayer and read the first and second drafts, as well as those who have been part of the editing process. I really appreciate all the time and effort you have put into bringing this book to publication. You know who you are, and I am internally grateful for your encouragement and belief in me.

Finally, I would like to give recognition to Levi Lusko's *Through the Eyes of a Lion*, which encouraged me to share my innermost feelings as I could resonate on so many levels when I read his book.

Prologue

My name is Marley Asher Adeshino Prescott, born on 3 December 2002.

"So cute," I heard my dad say, admiring my one-day-old self. So many eyes peered at me.

"He's a beautiful baby. He has such a small mouth; I hope he'll be able to latch on to the nipple."

These were all the lovely things that were being said about me two hours after my long-awaited arrival into this world. Well, I say long awaited—I was only two weeks over the due date, but to my mum and dad it felt like a long time.

I was loved and I felt it. I only had to cry for two seconds, and my big brother would be hovering over my carrycot, cooing at me with wide eyes.

"What's wrong, baby brother?" he would ask. "Are you hungry? Have you wet your nappy? Do you want to be picked up?"

My mum would come rushing from the kitchen to the living room. "What did you do to him? Did you try to pick him up?"

My mum would pick me up and I would stop crying. She would check my diaper to see if I was wet or had done a poo. If all was OK, she would check the clock to see what the time was and whether I was close to my next feed.

She seemed to know exactly what I needed: attention. She would get a toy and ask my big brother to play with me so she could finish cooking dinner before my dad got home. I was loved and I felt it.

When dad got home, he would pick me up and stare at me. A few days after my birth, I think he was still wondering how he could have produced such a beautiful baby with such a small mouth that could hardly latch on to the nipple to get enough milk when he was hungry.

"How is my ragamuffin?" he would ask.

Of course he knew I couldn't answer. I was only a few days old; I was trying to make sense of all the different noises, sounds, smells, and touches. I was still coming to terms with this new world. I was no longer in my mother's womb.

I had some work to do if my diaper needed changing or if I wanted some food, as, of course, I was no longer connected by the umbilical cord to an unlimited supply of nourishment.

I was loved and I felt it.

PART I

In Marley's View

1

School Days

A month after my 15th birthday, I was back at school after the Christmas holidays. I found it hard to adjust to going back because I had to face my peers at school. Meeting new people, no matter their age, was difficult for me. There was something about people staring at me, as if they could see into my thoughts or were making judgments about me.

I'd been trying to fit in at that school for four years, and still it was a struggle because I had no one I could call a friend. I had been let down so many times, and you would think I would have given up.

But no—I still had hopes that maybe, just maybe, someone would move from another school at the start of this term, connect with me, and become my friend. Children from families who had relocated to our area regularly joined my school. Maybe one would be the person I could hang out with during breaks, at lunchtime, and

1

even after school. Yes, I still had some dwindling hopes of having a friend after four years of attending this secondary school.

Usually, if it got to lunchtime on the first day of term and I hadn't connected with any of the newcomers, my hopes of making new friends would disappear. I would conclude that it was not to be, and my time at school would be the same old pattern again this term. I needed something to get me through these first days of school after the holidays.

It was Mum's habit to ask me how my day had been when I got home. This particular day was no different. "How was school today?" she asked.

I grunted something at her with a scowl on my face because when I got home, the last thing I wanted to be reminded of was school.

I wanted to forget about the teachers moving me from seat to seat when I did nothing to warrant it.

I wanted to forget about the kids who I thought were looking at me as if I was weird because I had no one to hang out with at breaks and lunch.

I wanted to forget about all the different subjects that were causing confusion in my mind.

It was hard to smile and give a fake answer to Mum. So I repeated what I'd been saying for four years. "You know exactly how school was—the same as it has been every day I go to that school. Bad. Every day is bad. This is the reason I've repeatedly asked you to move me to another school."

I stomped off to my room before she could respond, as it would be the same response she always gave: "It was too late to move you to another school; your GCSE exams are in just over twelve months, and it would unsettle you."

Blah, blah, blah.

"Who cares about GCSEs and exams?" I replied. Not me. I had bigger problems to sort out.

I reached my room and slammed the door. I knew I would be

left alone for at least the next two hours or so while she still worked. She worked from home when she wasn't traveling to other countries for her job.

I sneaked downstairs and reached for my secret bottle of lager that was chilling in the fridge. No one had caught on yet that the bottles of lager were disappearing. I could drink in peace and shut out my immediate problems of school, my lack of friends, and my parents moaning at me all the time. I'd probably fall asleep and wake up with a headache, but hey ho, at least I would have blanked things from my mind for a while and temporarily paused my nonstop thoughts about how I ended up with no friends.

I finished my lager thinking about what my life would be like if I had some friends—well, at least one—and with this in my mind, I fell into a dreamless sleep.

2

A Bottle or Two

I woke up suddenly, not knowing what had interrupted my sleep. Then I heard Mum saying, "Don't you want dinner? You've been sleeping since you came home from school, and it's now seven o'clock."

I had a piercing headache, and while I was still in that waking haze, I wondered what had caused it. Then I became fully awake and wondered if the bottle of lager was in view for her to see, having just realized she was in my room.

I looked around and didn't see any evidence of my drinking spree. Phew! That was lucky; I must have hidden the evidence. I grunted something to get her to leave and moaned that I had a headache. Little did she know that my headache was due to the lager I had drunk to numb the feelings of emptiness I had because of my lack of friends.

I managed to get her to leave, mumbling that I would be down soon for dinner. The pain in my head felt worse. I really needed some painkillers. I regretted drinking. I was now dealing with the aftereffects, and it wasn't pleasant. The relief from not thinking about my loneliness was only temporary. Now I had all those thoughts back in full force, along with a piercing headache and all the worry of someone finding out that I had been drinking. I needed to wash my mouth out and get some pain relief.

After rinsing my mouth to get rid of the alcohol smell, I searched for some gum and headed downstairs.

I checked what was for dinner and asked if I could have some paracetamol. As usual, she told me to have some dinner, which would get rid of the headache. In her opinion, I was too quick to take medication at the slightest hint of pain. I thought better than to argue with her, as I was hungry anyway and speaking only made my head hurt.

I had my dinner of pasta and mince, typical on Tuesdays. I knew exactly what the menu for each day would be, as Mum was predictable in that sense. Leftover Sunday dinner was always on the menu for Monday, and for some reason, pasta and mince was always on Tuesday, which I didn't mind, as I loved pasta. There was some sort of chicken dish with rice on Wednesday and beef on Thursday, while anything goes on Friday.

I loved Fridays for several reasons. Firstly, it was the end of the school week, and secondly, it was the day I could choose my meal; basically, I'd rummage in the freezer for pizza or chips and sausage, which I could put in the oven. The third reason I liked Friday was because I could stay up late on the computer, animating or playing games. I loved it. There was no pressure to go to bed since the next day was Saturday.

My head still hurt after dinner, so I approached her again for the elusive paracetamol. If she hadn't hidden the box, I would have helped myself as I had done in the past. I didn't have a high threshold for pain.

"Mum, could I have two paracetamols? I still have a headache," I said.

She looked at me and told me to go ask my dad. I hated asking him for anything; it was always a longer process than asking Mum.

"Dad won't know where the paracetamol is. Could you please get it?" I put on a sad face to get some sympathy. It worked, and she got me the medication.

I was glad. Soon I would be able to get rid of this headache. But if she only knew what was causing my headache, there would be an outrage. I made sure to get rid of the empty lager bottles before the cleaner came the following week. I didn't want her to find them when she cleaned my room.

That was my thinking, anyway. I didn't expect that by the end of the week I would be outed.

3

Outed 1

Friday had finally arrived; it was like a long-awaited friend. Because it was the end of the school week, junk food, such as pizza, chips, and sausage—or fish—awaited me when I got home. I pedaled fast after school to rush home.

I got home and noticed that my older brother was inside. I wondered what the occasion was before realizing that he had been home the day before too, because he had celebrated his birthday earlier in the week. He had a few days off work.

I quickly said hello to everyone and rushed off to my room, my haven.

The rest of the afternoon flew by. I decided to have pizza and some oven chips. I made my way downstairs after being on the Xbox for a while.

After having dinner, I was back in my room playing on my phone. Mom knocked on my door and came in. She always entered before I could tell her to come in. I guess she thought she didn't need my permission, and I always wondered why she bothered knocking anyway.

She took a seat on the chair where I usually sit when playing my Xbox and said, "You've drunk almost the whole box of lager that your brother received as a Christmas present from work. I want to know why."

I was stunned. I looked at her with a little smirk on my face. For some unknown reason I always had a smirk on my face no matter how serious the conversation I was having with my family. This usually angered them—they thought I didn't realise the seriousness of the discussion.

This evening was no exception. Mum raised her voice, getting angry. She told me it was illegal at my age to be drinking and asked again why I had drank almost a full box of lager.

All I could think to tell her was that since I didn't get any pocket money and I had a craving for fizzy drinks, this was the reason for my lager drinking. It was basically to satisfy my craving for fizz. I withheld all the other reasons, such as wanting to forget how alone I felt because I didn't have any friends, because I knew this would lead to discussions that I didn't want to have on this occasion.

To my surprise, all her anger seemed to evaporate. "Is that the only reason?"

"Yes," I said to close the matter. I would use this excuse and stick to it, because anything else would cause her to lose sympathy for me.

She said she'd make a deal with me to provide one can of fizzy drink every day to satisfy my craving as long as I promised that I wouldn't touch any more alcoholic drinks without her permission. She said she was aware that it wasn't only the bottles of lager that I had drunk but that I had helped myself to unfinished bottles of Cockspur, a rum from Barbados, and Martini, which were in the cupboard. I had lost count of the different bottles I had reached for in my moments of desperation.

Listening to her go on about the dangers of what I had done slowly brought it home to me that my actions had really disappointed her.

I had to do better. I promised I wouldn't touch any more alcohol. The fact that she had hidden whatever was left made it easy to keep the promise anyway. She had also promised to give me a can of fizzy drink, so if anything, I should be OK. But then I realised it wasn't over, because I knew I had to face my dad and brother.

"Does everyone know about this?" I asked.

"Yes," she responded, "but I told them to wait until I had spoken to you."

In my shock I had forgotten to ask these questions at the start. For some reason her answer made me really angry. I pictured them having full knowledge of what I had done, discussing it whilst I was at school, and greeting me as normal when I got home, even though they knew I had drunk the alcohol. I told her I would have preferred it if everyone had jumped on me as soon as I came through the door rather than keep me in the dark until now. It felt like they had been pretending that everything was OK.

It was Mum's turn to be stunned. She couldn't understand why I was angry. As she had said, she didn't want my dad and brother to jump on me as soon as I came home from school, because she knew how hard school was for me.

I was fuming and shouted at her. She couldn't understand how I felt, having been in this cocoon of comfort for several hours thinking no one knew what I had done, only to find out how wrong I was.

After she left, I immediately sought out my brother to lash out at him in anger. I'd forgotten that I was in the wrong.

He was ready for me. He let loose his anger at me for drinking almost all the lager he had received as a Christmas present. He told me that, as usual, I had got off lightly with Mum promising me fizzy drinks every day. I was oblivious as to how wrong my anger was considering what I had done. I felt justified in believing that my family had betrayed me, which led to my false sense that I was the victim of injustice.

My dad soon joined in the heated discussion, which didn't help matters. He was angry, and I was fuming, and we both had raised voices. Mum intervened by asking me to go to my room. I consented because I didn't want her to take away my cans of fizzy drink. I had let off some steam and could retreat to my room to play my Xbox. It was only Friday, and I wasn't looking forward to the rest of the evening. At least there would be one less person to contend with. My brother was going away with his friends to celebrate his birthday.

4

Holiday In Gambia

Looking back to the previous weekend, as much as I had dreaded constant references to the revelations of Friday night, it turned out to be nothing like that. Apart from a few comments here and there from my dad, which I ignored, all was back to normal for me.

I had come out of the situation with a better deal; getting one can of fizzy drink a day was something I hadn't expected, but I was happy about it.

School continued as normal—if you can call it that. There was nothing normal about it, but I was slowly coming to the realisation that there was nothing I could change. I would soon be leaving the school environment in a matter of months.

I was also looking forward to the Easter break as we were going on holiday to Gambia, a country in West Africa close to Sierra Leone, where my mum is from.

My auntie, who had looked after me when I was a baby, was also joining us in Gambia for the weeklong holiday. It had been two years since she left England to return to Sierra Leone for her daughter's wedding. I was looking forward to seeing her again.

Our time in Gambia was an eye opener. This was the first time I was faced with children my age and younger who had far less than I had. All the issues with school and lack of friends seemed to fade away in light of the abject poverty in which some of the children lived.

We also visited historical sites where captured slaves had been detained before being shipped to America and the Caribbean. I reflected on the suffering my ancestors had faced. It was mind-blowing seeing the cells and chains and hearing the guide narrate horrific stories of how some of these people met their deaths if they weren't strong or fit enough for the life that awaited them in their new destination.

I wasn't exactly empathetic. I had realised that I didn't feel strong emotions over the pain and suffering of others. Don't get me wrong; I wasn't heartless. But on this occasion, after hearing all these sad stories and seeing the evidence, I felt sorry for these people, and maybe because I had felt so lonely, I could relate to some of the despair and agony they had faced. I was moved to give away some of my spending money to the young boys and girls who were following us and begging for anything that we had. I gave away the sweets I had and was amazed at the jostling and fighting by more than twenty children who wanted them.

It made me think about the privileges I had. I was born into a family that had more than enough and didn't want for basic human needs. I had taken it for granted.

When I reflect on our holiday in Gambia, I know that I returned to England with some good feelings. I was a bit more appreciative and grateful for the life I had, even though it wasn't perfect. The good thing was that I still had some days of holiday before returning to school. I focused on playing Xbox live online and teaching myself animation. I was determined to complete my first video.

Around this time, Mum was planning a party for her 50th birthday, and the holiday to Gambia had been part of the year-long celebrations she had in mind. She asked me to put together a slideshow of the memorable events of the last twelve months and said that I could use this opportunity to launch my YouTube channel. I said I would think about it, but not because I didn't want to do it. I didn't want to be in the spotlight. Having all eyes on me was something I shied away from.

In the end, she asked my brother to do it since I kept telling her I would think about it. But I never took steps to do anything about it, and the day was fast approaching.

5

Friends and Private Tutor

In the weeks leading up to summer vacation, I found out that someone who was the closest I came to calling a friend was leaving the area because his parents had got a new job about two hundred miles north.

It's a funny thing when you realise you'll no longer have what you had. Suddenly you realise how much you'll miss it. The thought of this person moving—someone I hadn't realised was my only friend—was devastating. It's not that we were in the habit of hanging out after school on a regular basis, but I suddenly realised I wouldn't have that opportunity anymore.

I reached out to another boy who was a year below me at school. He was keen to hang out with me after school. For the first time in years, I felt that I had someone I could chill out with … especially when I realised he had access to alcohol and weed.

I was keen to hang out after school, and because I'd been

whinging for so long that I didn't have any friends, Mum was quick to say yes when I told her I'd be hanging out with some friends in the park and playing football. Little did she know what I was up to.

It was the much longed-for relief I was looking for: To be out of my room, not thinking about my sad situation of having no friends. I could forget my issues with the help of alcohol and weed whilst hanging out with my so-called friend. I say so-called because deep down, I knew it wouldn't last. He was from a different culture and younger than me, and I guessed that sooner or later his parents wouldn't want him hanging out with me. But while it lasted, I would make good use of the opportunity.

I was drowning my thoughts in alcohol and getting small bottles of vodka that I could smuggle into the house, which I could have when my thoughts tried to get the better of me. I didn't realise that this wasn't the way to deal with my problems, but I couldn't help myself.

Before the start of the new term, my so-called friend had been grounded by his older brother, who told him not to hang out with me; he thought I was a bad influence. Little did he know his brother was the bad influence.

This made me dread the start of the new school term and my final year. I had nothing to look forward to. I put renewed pressure on Mum for a transfer, although there was zero chance of this happening. The previous attempt had been unsuccessful.

Mum secured a private tutor for Mathematics and English but soon realised my efforts should be focused on Mathematics. I was so far behind the syllabus compared to where I should be. I tried to give time and effort to mathematics, but there was too much going on in my head that I couldn't understand. What was the point of trying to explain it to others? All the homework I was given by my private tutor was untouched until the next time we met, and this was really annoying for her. My mind wandered, so I couldn't focus on practising the stuff we had studied when I was on my own. I really tried to concentrate and give attention to it. Mum kept reminding me how much it cost to have a private tutor twice a week.

Despite my efforts appearing minimal to others, I thought I was doing a lot. No one knew what I was going through day in, day out, just dealing with all the thoughts in my head.

After several lessons of untouched homework, my tutor finally gave up. She told Mum that it was a waste of time; I just wasn't interested. Every piece of homework she gave me I hadn't done, and whatever we did during the previous lesson she would have to go through all over again.

In her opinion it was a waste of money. It would be better to stop now than to waste more money on private tutoring. Even though she was getting paid, at the end of the day I would have nothing to show for it. I guess she was also concerned about her reputation. She didn't want to get a review that indicated she spent a year tutoring me and I still didn't get a good grade in my GCSE in mathematics.

In a way I was happy, but at the same time I wasn't. I knew Mum would be upset and angry about how much she had spent on private tuition, especially if I didn't get the grades in my forthcoming examination.

6

Early School Years

Sometimes I wonder how I ended up the way I am—wanting friends but not having any, or pushing away people who had tried to befriend me because they weren't meeting my expectations of what a friend should be.

I think I was happy for the first ten years of my life. I never had to deal with staying at different houses with different child minders, which other young children experienced at an early age. My parents had invited a close family friend from Africa, the auntie who reunited with us on our Gambian holiday, to live with us. She came over when I was a baby to look after me and my brother, since my parents worked full time.

My brother and I were never shuffled from one house to another after school or during school holidays. My auntie took me to playgroup when I was little since Mum didn't want me to go to nursery until I could go to preschool. Later, in my teens, I had asked her if the reason I was finding it hard to make friends was because I hadn't gone to nursery. I had grown up being more comfortable on my own.

She disagreed, saying that I had an older brother. Although he was about three years older than me and there wasn't much of an age gap between us, I had always preferred playing on my own. I would play for hours with my toys because sometimes what I wanted to do was different to what my brother wanted to do. This led to me being quite content to play by myself. Even when I did make friends at preschool, I could easily leave them whilst I went to another room to play by myself.

I knew my auntie might have thought that was odd, but to me it was fine. That gave my brother the freedom to do what he wanted while I had the freedom to do what I wanted. That was the way I saw it, and many, including Mum, didn't agree with me, but it was OK.

Even when we went on holiday for the first time, I only wanted to play or hang out with my brother. But being the social butterfly he was, there were always other children competing for his attention. I had realised at that early age that I wasn't going to compete and would therefore leave him with his new friends and play by myself.

Nevertheless, whether it was from spending long days alone with my auntie whilst my parents went to work and my brother went to school, I had developed the art of living within my head. I expressed myself through my Lego toys.

When I started preschool, boys and girls wanted to be my friends, but I was overwhelmed and shied away.

One girl wouldn't give up and pulled me into her circle of friends. After school, we happily walked along with my auntie and her mum when they picked us up from school. It was a bag of mixed emotions: lovely on one hand that someone wasn't put off by my awkward and shy disposition, but on the other hand, I felt a bit intimidated. I couldn't say no when she pulled me along during playtime or heading home after school.

Eventually, I was bold enough to break away from her circle of girls and make my own friends. I probably learnt a thing or two from her; I became the bold one in my newly found group of three friends. I dictated what games we played and basically used the tricks I had learnt from my first girlfriend, as I liked to call her. I moved from preschool into the first year of school with this group. I made sure no one could break our tight group of three. I kept out any other boys or girls who tried to join us. I was happy, but I didn't realise it wasn't going to last beyond lower school.

7

Enjoying Life

The first ten years of my life were the happiest. I was the leader of a close circle of friends. I dictated what we did at school and after school. My closest friend stayed at my house until his parents picked him up after work.

Shyness aside, I was in a happy place. I could play on my own if that was the mood I was in, or I could play with my close friend or my brother. My brother also had a close friend who was the son of one of my mum's closest friends. We went places together as a trio with our parents.

Every half-term holiday or during the main school holidays, we went to the cinema to watch the latest animated movies. We got popcorn and other snacks and munched our way through the movies. I watched movies such as *Shrek, The Incredibles, Wreck-It Ralph, Up*, and many others. We also rented movies on video or DVD, and they were the last thing we watched before going to bed.

My brother and I had bunkbeds. I had the bottom bunk until he got bigger, and then we swapped. Those were good days as we fought and made up. Mainly we argued over what to watch. I usually won, because as soon as Mum heard us, she took my side because I was younger. She told my brother to look after me and give me the first choice, and then we watched what he wanted.

It was fun because we had our own telly and DVD player, so we could control what we watched. Our parents hardly bothered us when we said goodnight and went to bed. During those nights we also sneaked biscuits and crisps into our bedroom by hiding them in our pants when going upstairs.

Most of the time we got away with it, but sometimes I would give away that something was in my pants because I walked funny. Mum asked why I was walking funny and then discovered the biscuits or other snacks. I would lose my snacks and get told off. By then we would already have brushed our teeth, which meant no more food or drinks.

As we got older, we sneaked movies from our parents' collection, which we weren't allowed to watch. But there was something about watching a forbidden movie that we couldn't resist. On occasions, we had my brother's friend for a sleepover, and we all had so much fun. Whilst this friend was the same age as my brother, he treated me as if I was their age We wrestled and tumbled about, and sometimes when it got too noisy, my dad would tell us off.

On other occasions we went to the park to play football, have fun on the slides, or ride our bikes. Other times we went on trips to theme parks or animal farms for the whole day.

Other times, my school friend's parents asked Mum and Dad if I could join them on a family trip. On such an occasion we went to Winter Wonderland, and I ate a nice juicy hotdog. That was a memorable day. Another time we went to Thorpe Park, and I was able to go on most of the rides because I met the height requirement.

One of the highlights of those early years was going away on my first holiday to Tunisia with my family, my close friend, and his family. I was a baby or very young on previous holidays and couldn't remember what had gone on. So, when Mum arranged with my friend's mum that we should all go on holiday to Tunisia, I was very excited. We arrived in Tunisia very late after flying from Birmingham airport.

My brother and I had our own room with ensuite, and it made us feel grown up, although there was a connecting door to our parents' room. We spent a lot of time in the pool, and although I wasn't a good swimmer, I had floaters, which made me feel protected and safe.

Sometimes during the day there were activities led by the entertainment team. We could participate or we could just sit on our loungers and enjoy the show. On other occasions, we went on a day trip organised by the hotel. On one of these trips, my dad and I rode a camel. Although it was very smelly, the experience of being so far from the ground on an animal I had only seen on telly was thrilling.

What I enjoyed most on this particular holiday were the evenings when we would have a change of clothes for dinner, and I could choose what I wanted to eat and had access to unlimited fizzy drinks since we had wristbands indicating that we were part of an all-inclusive package.

After dinner we either went for a walk to explore the surrounding area or stayed at the hotel to watch an evening show. Either option was fine by me; it meant we were staying out late and not going to bed early, which was the norm when we were at home.

We discovered I was allergic to one of the ingredients in the sun lotion Mum had bought for us to use. It was about the third day of our holiday when I woke up with one side of my face really puffed up. My mum and dad were quite concerned and got a doctor to examine me. I was prescribed some medication to fight the allergic reaction, and over the coming day or two the puffiness slowly reduced. Once the puffiness disappeared, I was back to spending a lot of time in the pool—without sun cream.

We already knew my brother and I were allergic to nuts, but we had never been tested, so getting this reaction from the sun lotion was something else to worry about.

It was an enjoyable holiday, and one I remembered for a long time. Finally, I could go back to school, tell my friends all about it, and I was able to write in my English class about what I had done whilst on holiday.

8

Allergy and Orlando

Due to the allergic reaction, I had in Tunisia, Mum decided to get me tested for allergies. Unfortunately, before the appointment I had another incident whilst away on an overnight school trip. I hadn't taken any sun lotion with me as Mum knew that I had reacted to it. But a teacher decided to put sun cream on me, and I immediately reacted to it with the same puffiness on one side of my face.

The teacher was extremely alarmed and made a phone call to Mum. I was immediately sent back home with a teacher, and that was the first and last overnight trip I did during my time at school. I hated the unnecessary focus on me and the attention from all the teachers. If Mum was having any doubt about me being tested, this incident confirmed that she needed to get it done.

I was taken to the doctor, who referred me to the hospital. My mum was asked to prepare different cookies following a recipe sent by the hospital. Each cookie had a different type of nut in it, and this tested my reaction. I was a bit concerned because on the odd occasion when we'd been to parties and I'd had a bite of food containing some type of nut, my lips would become swollen whilst my throat got very scratchy. My mum assured me that since I would be tasting them in a controlled environment in the hospital, I'd be fine.

When we arrived at hospital, I thought it would be over quickly. I had visions of finishing early and getting home to play my games. Unfortunately, it was almost an all-day event. Each cookie with the different type of nut was tested individually. Some I had to have a little bite and then be observed. With others the cookie was put on my skin and any reaction noted. I was pleasantly surprised that I wasn't allergic to almonds or hazelnuts. I had a strong reaction to peanuts, which wasn't a surprise at all. I also had a strong allergy to Brazil, cashew, and pistachio nuts.

I had one up on my brother. I could eat any chocolates with almonds or hazelnuts in them without fear of an allergic reaction, but because he hadn't been tested, he had to stay away from all nuts.

Not too long after my testing, Mum told me our next holiday would be in Orlando, Florida. I'd been asking for this trip for what seemed like forever. Although I enjoyed the holiday to Tunisia, the one I enjoyed the most was in Orlando.

In the summer of 2012, we went to Orlando. My mum always said I was fearless. I was raring to go on roller coasters, no matter how high or scary they were. I loved the adrenaline rush.

I counted down the days to our holiday in Orlando. We had to go to Gatwick the day before as the flight was leaving quite early in the morning, and since we were taking the train, we didn't want to risk missing our flight.

We were also travelling with another family of six, which included four boys—three of whom were around the same age as me. I thought it might be good to have young people to talk to instead of strangers.

The hotel wasn't the same as the one we had in Tunisia. It wasn't all-inclusive. My mum said the holiday was expensive as we were there for about ten days, so we had to go for a cheaper hotel. I didn't mind as long as we had the passes for all the rides. There was also a pool at the hotel where we spent time cooling off when it was too hot.

On the first day we went to Walt Disney World, and I was a bit disappointed. It wasn't what I was expecting. It was more for little kids, but our parents thought we should experience all that we had paid for, so I had no choice but to put up with this kiddie stuff until we could go to the bigger rides. I was looking forward to Universal Studios Hollywood.

Over the next ten days we visited all the famous theme parks I had heard so much about from kids in school who had already been on holiday to Florida. I was able to go on most of the rides because I met the height requirements. There were some rides my brother couldn't go on because he suffers from motion sickness, but for me, the higher and faster the experience, the better it was.

We also had some trips to the shopping mall when Mum said to choose some trainers, T-shirts, and any souvenirs we wanted to take back with us. We attended some shows and had dinner at different restaurants, and I met one of my cousins who I had never met before because she lived in Florida with her husband. They joined us for drinks one evening at our hotel.

There were other holidays we went on during the next six years, but none was more enjoyable than our Orlando holiday.

9

Life in Church

Mum was very spiritual, and every Sunday we went to church, although Dad only came on special occasions, such as Christmas, Father's Day, or Easter. From a young age I remember going to Little and Loud, which was Sunday school for young children. It would be wrong to say I didn't like it, but I used to cry, and sometimes the Sunday school teacher would get Mum from the service. It was more a case of not wanting to be amongst other children that I didn't know. I wanted to be with Mum and my auntie, and I didn't want to get to know other children. It would have been better if I was left on my own to play with the toys and didn't have to mix with the others. Gradually, as I got older, I became more settled but still wouldn't say much at Sunday school.

One of my Sunday school teachers, who was a friend of Mum's, would say how quiet I was and always looked out for me, trying to get me to say something or to join in the activities. Around this time, I realised I liked drawing and could get lost sketching different cartoons and pictures. Whenever we had activities that included drawing or something to do with art, I was happy to immerse myself in it. My parents and auntie told me I had a talent, and even my brother told me I was really good. For me it was just something I liked doing and that I could get engrossed in.

Church in those early days was somewhere I went on Sundays because Mum wanted me to go. With time, I used it to get something I had developed a love for: McDonald's. We stopped there to get something for lunch so Mum or my auntie didn't have to prepare something at home. On other occasions we left church later and stopping by McDonald's for lunch became the norm. Mum soon realised it was a way of getting me to go to church.

I had outgrown the younger Sunday school classes but didn't want to go to the over-twelves class. At the same time, I found sitting in church with all the adults boring, so I made excuses not to go to church, especially when my older brother decided he didn't want to go every Sunday but only on special occasions.

I was asked to play Joseph in the Christmas nativity on the Sunday before Christmas. I didn't want to do it—I was nervous about being up on stage and having all those people staring at me—but I accepted. We practiced in Sunday school at first, and Mum was told what the dress code was for the role of Joseph on the day. I think it was two weeks before the Nativity when I caught chickenpox. Whilst it was uncomfortable, I thought it would get me out of the Nativity; someone else could take my place. My mum, on the other hand, wasn't having it. She must have been longing for one of us to be given such a leading role. She got this white stuff to put on my spots. My auntie, who knew all the traditional remedies from Sierra Leone, put forward some solutions so that I would be ready for my part as Joseph.

I realised I wasn't cut out to be in the limelight. I was uncomfortable with it.

Years later, my brother teased me whenever we saw the girl who had played the part of Mary and said, "There goes your Mary!"

I would get annoyed and say, "She's not my Mary."

I knew I was no actor and preferred to be behind the scenes. As if my stint in a nativity wasn't enough, Mum decided to enrol my brother and me in a Saturday drama school. It seemed she was determined to make an actor out of me. At first it was fun to be out of the house on a Saturday, taking a walk up the road to the drama school, which was about ten minutes from our house.

But it was no longer fun when the drama teacher decided I was to play a part in the production in which my older brother had a starring role. I started dreading going to drama school and told my auntie and Mum I didn't want to do it. I was so stressed out about it that Mum had to speak to the teacher to let her know I was no longer going to be part of it. Again, I realised I didn't like being in the spotlight whilst my brother seemed to love it.

Surprisingly, I didn't have a problem being part of the school Christmas production. During my years at my lower school there were many occasions when I was part of a group performance, and my parents, and sometimes my nan and my auntie, would be invited to school to watch.

My brother and I also attended Friday Night Club at church, but that didn't last long. After a full day of school, I wasn't always in the mood to be around people I didn't know, even though my brother would also be there. One incentive for going to the Friday Night Club was the access to sweets and junk food. Though Mum let us have fizzy drinks or sweets, it was only on special occasions (until later, after the lager incident). I had discovered from an early age when attending friends' birthday parties that I loved anything sugary.

I say "friends" loosely because, in those days, you didn't have to be a close friend. The whole class would be invited to a birthday party because that was the thing to do. If Mum was free and I had some interactions with the birthday boy or girl, then I would attend, but Mum didn't see the point of spending money and effort if I never played with the person who had invited me.

On the occasions when I got an invite to a McDonald's party, of course I would tell Mum that I played with the person during lunchtime just so I could go to McDonald's! I didn't mind going to parties that were held at a local place called Snakes and Ladders; it was a play centre where you could do your own thing.

I wouldn't say I was a loner, but I definitely didn't like to be around too many people. I preferred one or two people. Even when it was my birthday and Mum wanted me to invite friends from school, I preferred just a few from school, the friends I knew outside school, and my cousins.

10

Something about December

One of my favourite times of the year (apart from the summer holidays) was December. My birthday was at the start of December, and, of course, there were the Christmas holidays, decorating the house, putting up the Christmas tree and lights, and, of course, getting birthday and Christmas presents.

I usually made a list of what I wanted for my birthday and for Christmas. This way Mum knew what was urgent and what could wait until Christmas. I always chose games and games console. I hardly asked for clothes and just wasn't bothered about things like that. In December 2016, the list for my birthday was Dragon Ball Xenoverse 2 video game for Xbox One, WWE 2K17 video game for Xbox, and a graphic/drawing tablet.

For Christmas, the list consisted of a Google Pixel phone, money, and a laptop. I got everything on my birthday list but got other things for Christmas. Mum didn't think I needed an expensive

Google phone since I had a reputation for breaking most of the electronics I owned. I didn't get the laptop either because I used the desktop PC in the house. I wanted the convenience of having a laptop that I could take to my bedroom, especially at night. I knew I wouldn't get the money on my list—Mum never gave us money for Christmas (except pocket money, which was rather random, and it was the first thing to go if we did something wrong).

Even when I decided I didn't want to take a packed lunch to school and preferred to buy food at school, she gave me lunch money every day instead of weekly. It was a pain, but there was nothing I could do about it.

After my birthday, the following weekend we put up the Christmas decorations. Mum always asked me to help with the Christmas tree decorations, whilst my brother helped Dad with the lights in the front garden. I asked for some lights in my bedroom window and in the front windows of the house. It was my job to turn the lights on and off when I was younger. I loved seeing the house all lit up in the evening.

When we were younger, my parents took me and my brother to Toys"R"Us during December so we could get a gift for each other. We split up. I usually went with Mum, my brother with Dad. At first I was more concerned with getting something for myself; the store was full of so many things I would have loved to have. Our parents told my brother and me that we needed to think of others and not just about ourselves, but once I got inside, I couldn't think of anything except for what I could get for myself. I'm sure it was a stressful time for our parents, especially the few occasions when I was paired off with my dad.

Eventually something meant to be fun would end up with me in tears because I didn't get what I wanted. I'm glad my behaviour didn't put Mum off. The following year we were back in the store doing it all over again—after convincing Dad that it was worth it.

Another December memory was the smell of Christmas cake being baked in the oven. Every year Mum baked this traditional

Christmas cake (which Caribbean people call black cake)—a rich cake prepared with fruits soaked in rum. I think I got a little tipsy eating it! The smell of cinnamon, nutmeg, and vanilla pulled me downstairs. I longed for a taste. I was only given a small piece, but later I helped myself when no one was around.

The smell of the cooked ham and turkey on Christmas Day was one of my favourite times. We usually went to church as a family in the morning. I looked forward to singing "The Twelve Days of Christmas", when all the males in church stood up for the odd numbers and all the women stood up for the even numbers. It was definitely a highlight of Christmas Day before we got home and opened our presents.

11

Paperboy

I can't say exactly when it started, but I know that at the end of 2018 or the beginning of 2019, I was fed up with school. Maybe it wasn't just school though, because I even seemed to have lost the joy I felt when the weekend was approaching. Going to school was a chore, and my GCSEs were starting in May. I was nowhere close to where I should be with my grades, and I was under pressure to do well so I could go to college and study animation, which was the only thing I enjoyed doing these days.

I constantly told Mum I wasn't happy and that every school day was a bad day. I just didn't get any pleasure from being at school. It got so bad that Mum took me to the doctor again to get a referral because I was all over the place. I couldn't help talking back and arguing with anyone who asked me how I was after I got home from school. I knew I was a nightmare, but I couldn't do anything about it.

The doctor told us to get the school to refer me for outside support since I didn't want anyone in school to know my business. I had seen how other children who needed support were ridiculed and I had enough on my plate without adding this too. I was given a letter to take to the person responsible for school pastoral care. This was a task in itself. I didn't want to be seen with this particular teacher; if someone saw me, schoolmates would know and would conclude there was something wrong with me.

On the day I was supposed to meet with pastoral care, Mum kept phoning me. The teacher had given specific instructions as to where and when I should meet her to do the referral, but I hadn't turned up. As much as I wanted to get the referral done, there were too many people around who could see me, so I didn't go.

After two days of Mum pushing me to speak to the teacher, I finally had the meeting with her. She tried to tell me I could receive support in school, but I said I would prefer it to be external. She finally agreed and wrote a letter recommending outside organisations.

I believed this was the end of it, since I now had a piece of paper that said I was suffering from anxiety due to my forthcoming GCSEs. I figured I didn't need to see anyone else in or outside school. My mum was having none of it. She insisted I take the opportunity to address my ongoing issues; daily complaints about school, my lack of friends, inability to maintain friendships, and my growing social anxiety.

I got to the point where it made me really anxious if family and friends were coming round. I didn't want to visit family, and I didn't look forward to family gatherings at our house. I usually felt awkward at any gathering, whether it was close family members or not. I was okay with my immediate family, but with anyone else, it was difficult to socialise.

I would go on about it for days or weeks before the event, especially if I was the last to find out because I spent so much time in my room. I definitely needed professional help although I didn't want it.

After a lot of persuasion, Mum convinced me to take a call from an organisation supporting children and young people with anxiety disorders. I was asked several questions and tried to answer truthfully, although I didn't want to tell them everything I thought and felt. I didn't believe anyone would understand—sometimes conversations with my brother or Mum went round in circles. They didn't understand how or why I felt the way I did. I didn't understand it myself, so how could I explain it to anyone else? I figured if my immediate family couldn't understand me, what were the chances someone who didn't even know me would understand?

After about three or four telephone consultations I was given six sessions to attend at their local office with a dedicated consultant. I wasn't looking forward to it at all. I'm not a talker, especially with someone I don't know.

But just before I started attending these sessions, I had a breakthrough in another area. Since I was 13, I tried to get a job as a paperboy. I regularly spoke to the guy who owned the shop asking him to give me a chance. At first I was below the age requirements, and later, when I was old enough, there were no openings.

I wanted a bit of independence. My brother was working as an apprentice in a local component firm and could buy whatever he wanted. I wanted to earn some pocket money and not be so dependent on my parents for everything

Finally, around the Easter holidays, one of the girls with a regular paper round was going on holiday, and the newsagent asked me if I could cover her for a week. I was so excited; it felt like such a big achievement. My mum was really pleased, although both my parents had reservations about whether I would be able to do it successfully. I wasn't known as an early riser and sometimes ran late for school. This job would mean I had to get up extremely early—earlier than when I got ready for school—to be at the shop to collect the papers and deliver them.

I also had to follow a specific route to ensure that I delivered the papers to the correct houses. I had to shadow the girl before she went on holiday, and it was one of those awkward situations with me not saying much because I didn't know what to say.

On the Saturday morning for my trial, I woke up early, even though I had asked Mum to wake me up. That was just a backup plan in case I overslept.

My trial run was an eye-opener. There were about thirty-six houses on my round to deliver newspapers, and they were scattered all over the area where we lived. I soon realised I needed a bag that would be easily accessible to extract the papers whilst still enabling me to ride my bike. I also needed to remember all the addresses to which I was delivering; putting a paper through the wrong letter box wasn't acceptable.

Mistakes meant deductions from my earnings. I had proper responsibility. It was my first trial job, and I was determined to succeed. I had to prove to my parents and myself that I could do this. I arrived home a little exhausted, trying to work out my plan of action—the following Monday I would have to do this by myself.

On Monday I made mistakes and had some wages deducted because the shop owner had to correct my errors. After a few days it got better, and I understood what I needed to do. This was the beginning of my independence. My trial paper route was successful, and after I finished my GCSEs, the shop owner gave me a permanent round. I was ecstatic. I had a regular income to spend on what I liked and no longer needed to ask my parents for everything.

12

No More School

The excitement of being offered the paper round was short-lived as I soon had to sit my exams, which I was ill-prepared for. I even lacked the motivation to complete tasks for my artwork, which wasn't normal. Art was my thing.

Even though my parents had tried to incentivise me with money if I achieved certain grades, it still didn't push me to do more. I constantly got into trouble with the art teacher. She chased me to bring in my completed work, and in the end, she reached out to Mum, who of course insisted I complete the work that very evening so I could take it into school.

Did I do my best? Definitely not! I was at that point where I needed to get the teacher and Mum off my back, so I quickly did work that would pass as completed and handed it in. If you asked me why I didn't put in the effort, I couldn't give you an answer. But my head definitely wasn't in the right place. This was more evidence that I needed the outside support—which I was resisting.

I started attending the talking therapy sessions after finishing my GCSEs. Around the same time, there was the Leaver's Dance, which I had decided I wouldn't attend. I didn't see the point—I didn't have any friends, and I always felt awkward at such gatherings, so why torture myself? I was happy to receive some money from Mum. She told me she would give me one hundred pounds. It was part of the money she would have spent on me if I had gone to the Leaver's Dance. I kept some of it and used the other half on my favourite junk food.

Finally, I was a school leaver! I no longer had to go to the school I had hated for the last five years. I didn't have to see the people I didn't want to see. I felt I could do what I wanted. I was also aware that I needed to do something to get me out of the house. I still had the paper round, which was a couple of hours early in the morning each day. I needed something where I could interact with people on my own terms at a level that I could manage.

My brother helped me create my CV, and I applied for a lot of summer jobs, one at McDonald's. I wanted to do a job on my own terms. I thought I could apply for any job and then at the interview make it clear I only wanted part-time hours—even if the job was advertised as being full-time. Obviously, this became a big stumbling block.

I was determined to be out of the house, even if it meant volunteering at the local charity shop. I got an application form and was successful in being taken on. I had put on the form that I wanted tasks that involved sorting out the donated items so I would be in the background. I wasn't prepared for any customer-facing. It wasn't my thing. My worst nightmare would be working on the tills and speaking to customers.

The first two days went better than expected. I was in the back room sorting out CDs and DVDs that had been donated. I had limited interaction with people, which was fine by me. The third day didn't go so well. I was told the day before that I would be put on the till so I could cover in case the regular person wasn't in. I dreaded it. I considered stopping altogether. After a pep talk from Mum and my brother I decided to at least try once.

I arrived on the day and was shown what I needed to do. One of the senior volunteers would be with me during my shift. It was difficult for me as my anxiety kicked in. My palms grew sweaty, and my heart pounded as if I was running a hundred metres a minute. I felt stressed and didn't want to do it anymore. Although I had done a session with my support worker, who gave me coping mechanisms and tips to overcome these feelings, I realised I couldn't remember anything I had been told. I tried, but it was making me miserable, so I stopped volunteering at the charity shop.

Around the same time, I got an interview with McDonald's, but I was beginning to think this wouldn't work. I would be around people all the time and would feel awkward and uncomfortable. I went to the interview so that my parents and brother wouldn't be annoyed with me for not trying, but I knew deep down that it wasn't a job I would feel comfortable doing. I guess I didn't put a great deal of effort into the interview.

My dad dropped me off in the town centre, but my anxiety was already kicking in just thinking about the interview. I didn't recognise where I was and had to call Mum, who gave me directions. I arrived late to the interview.

I was asked if I was available seven days a week as that was what had been advertised. I told the woman I could only do Friday to Sunday. I didn't get the job. After this I gave up trying to get a summer job.

Soon after, the GCSE results were out, and I didn't get the grades I needed to go to college and study animation. I felt my life spiralling out of my control. If I couldn't get a job at McDonald's or cope with volunteering at the charity shop, what would I do for a living? What would my future look like? These questions kept churning round and round in my head, and I had no answer. I focussed on teaching myself animation and creating videos for my YouTube channel. I saw this as the only way for a future career.

When Mum asked me to retake some of my GCSEs, I told her I didn't need to go to college to be formally trained as I could teach myself.

Around this time, I decided I didn't want to continue with the help I was getting from the support worker. I didn't want to reveal some of the thoughts I was having. I told Mum that I wouldn't attend the last two sessions and used the excuse that the support worker had changed one of the session dates because he was going on vacation.

I was having a constant battle with Mum. She wouldn't let me get away with not attending some sort of studies to try to get back on track. I told her I needed a break until the end of 2019. After all, I was still recovering from all the stress I had dealt with at school.

She agreed but wanted me to attend an animation workshop, which included a week staying at a residential centre and then three weekends of sessions. I was interested, but the idea of being away from home and staying with strangers for a whole week didn't appeal to me.

It's funny that I had now become this antisocial person, when a few years back I was constantly begging Mum to look for an animation club I could attend. This was around the time when I realised that I wasn't into football and had no interest in all the different types of afterschool sport clubs—unlike my brother, who was involved with an under-14s football club at the time.

13

Who Wants Therapy?

It was a cold January morning. We had just landed back in England after seven nights in Freetown, Sierra Leone. I was glad to be back in my own safe space. Seven days of putting on a smiley face had left me with aching face muscles. I could go back to my routine of paper round, animation, Xbox Live games, and online games, such as Habbo, which I enjoyed. No more meeting family members I didn't know and would probably never see again. I felt relieved.

We got home, and Mum was immediately on my back to empty out my suitcase. She had put her stuff and things for other people in it. Whilst taking stuff out, I pulled out the outfit and souvenirs from my auntie, the one who had looked after me from the time I was a baby until I was 12, when she decided to go back to Sierra Leone for her daughter's wedding. I thought about the day we spent with her. It was definitely one of the highlights of my time in Sierra

Leone. She always cared about me, and to a certain extent I think I was her favourite. I wondered if I would ever get to see her again. It wasn't as if I made a habit of taking that long journey to Freetown.

I hadn't wanted to go in the first place. The thought of all those people—young and old, ones I knew and didn't know—all in one place and all looking at me filled me with dread. I was protesting for the eleven months before we even had our first jabs that I didn't want to go to Sierra Leone.

I know I caused Mum a lot of stress by being uncooperative about the general preparations for the trip. I couldn't make up my mind what clothes I needed to take. Some were too small, and I only told Mum this a few days before we were due to travel. I was also missing sliders and swimwear. Who can blame me? I didn't want to go, so I was being difficult every step of the way. If she could have seen inside my head, and if she had known the number of times I had to calm myself by taking stuff I had no business taking, she would have left me in England.

She kept saying, "You're having a holiday in a hot sunny place, staying in a hotel on the beach, with all expenses taken care of, and you don't want to go? Who would say no to that?"

If only she knew the thoughts going through my head, she would have cancelled the whole trip and got me to a psychiatrist. Just kidding—it wasn't *that* bad. She knew I had a serious case of anxiety about being in social gatherings and meeting new people, so of course going to my cousin's wedding would accelerate my anxiety attacks.

Anyway, that was all behind me now. It was a new year, and I was thinking about my future and my future plans. I knew that sooner or later, the topic of retaking my GCSEs or going to college or something would crop up. Just thinking about it depressed me. I had finished school, and here I was with nothing to show for it. My only way out was the animation videos I was creating and uploading to my YouTube channel. I wanted to get more likes and subscribers, but it was moving really slow.

I was becoming the hermit Mum had accused me of becoming, because I was hardly out of my room. Once I returned from my paper round and got breakfast, I retreated into my room and stayed there until evening. I only came out to get dinner. Sometimes Mum would come looking for me, but mostly I was left alone. They knew I would only get annoyed if someone came into my room.

Mum must have picked up something from my behaviour because she told me I needed to speak to someone. She said I was most likely depressed. I probably was, but I wouldn't admit it. I didn't want to speak to anyone. Part of me was afraid I'd spill out the dark thoughts running through my head, and then I might be labelled as troubled or mad or something. How many times had I shared some of my thoughts and then been asked what was wrong with me by one family member or another? I was only saying what was on my mind. I had a telephone appointment, which I knew I needed to accept if I wanted my favourite food. Mum definitely knew how to bribe me. I had no choice. I had to participate in the call, but I also prepared myself for what I would say. I didn't want to give away too much. I had to keep my guard up at all times.

14

Outed 2

A week later I was diagnosed with mild depression and offered ten counselling sessions with a therapist. I didn't want to attend. I felt it would be like the other support I had experienced in my last year of school. Unless I was prepared to open up and tell them everything that was going on in my head, it would be useless.

My mum, of course, had other ideas. She felt that I needed to speak to someone and told me to take it one session at a time. She sensed my unwillingness to do even one session, let alone ten.

I only attended one session, because then we were in lockdown due to the Covid-19 pandemic. The prime minister had announced that no social interaction was permitted outside our immediate household.

For me, it was the ideal situation. I no longer had to attend family events or visit aunties and uncles. We all had to stay in our own space. I loved it, not realising that it was slowly making me

45

worse. At least when family visited, it forced me to interact, to be social. In this situation I could just stay in my room and only make appearances at mealtimes.

My mum wasn't having it, though. She constantly tried to get me to go out into the garden for family barbecues or al fresco breakfast or something or the other. I was resisting all the way. I became withdrawn, barely spoke to my family unless I wanted something, and was flippant and obnoxious when anyone tried to ask me about anything I had done wrong.

I was also speaking to online contacts, asking opinions about different topics that I felt I couldn't discuss with anyone who knew me. I had withdrawn from my cousins and family friends, so I didn't share how I was feeling with them. My mum continued to try to get me to do more sessions with the therapist. I told her I was all right; I didn't need any more sessions. Sometimes she left me alone, but after a few weeks she would be back on my case. I was irritated, especially when she smelt weed on my clothes, my source of temporary relief, and what I'd been trying to hide came to light.

She was certain I had the weed in my room and insisted I give it to her. She took my laptop, which I had bought with my paper round money.

"Until you give me the weed you have hidden in your room, you won't get your laptop back," she threatened.

I'd underestimated her sense of smell. I realised I needed stronger air freshener to disguise it. I had checked online how to disguise the smell, but obviously it wasn't enough. I was really angry at that point and felt this overwhelming dislike for her. In fact, not just for her, but for my whole family.

"Why are you so against weed? It helps me, and it's only for recreational use," I said.

In the end I gave her the weed to get my laptop back. I knew she would destroy it, but what choice did I have?

The anger I felt later when I thought about what had happened really frightened me. I realised that I could have hit her, and that would have been unforgivable. What was happening to me? It was only weed. I used it to dull the thoughts in my head, and I had bought it with my own money. The laptop was purchased with my paper round money. She had no right to take these things away from me, I reasoned within myself. I was fuming. I needed to put an end to this.

I knew someone had been snooping around my room—one of my lighters was missing. I wanted to call them out, but how would I explain why I was in possession of the lighter? I couldn't, so I let it go and became even more withdrawn. I lacked privacy even in my own home.

I would barely greet Mum because I was still consumed with anger. I didn't speak to my dad, and I hardly said two words to my brother. I felt like they were all against me and I was on my own.

I was constantly doing things that annoyed them. It's not that I was going out of my way to be obnoxious, it was more about me not caring. I would leave things out of the fridge or not clean up after I made a mess. I constantly put food in the oven and retreated to my room until someone shouted for me to come get it, which really annoyed my parents.

When I was being told off for what I had done, I had a habit of walking away whilst Mum or Dad was speaking, and this aggravated the situation even more. I couldn't seem to help myself.

In the midst of all the angst I had against my family, I was especially angry with my dad. Don't ask me why; I couldn't tell you if I tried. Maybe it's because Mum seemed to have more patience with me.

Dad was great at baking. He made really delicious cakes, such as sweet bread, sponge cakes, and other really yummy stuff. I would be in my room and the smell of it would get me downstairs to investigate. Later, when all the goodies were laid out and no one was around, I helped myself. I would later get told off because I had eaten it all without thinking that others might not have had any. At the same time, I was constantly saying sorry to Mum or texting her with apologies after I'd had time to calm down and reflect on the situation. Deep down I knew I was at fault, but I couldn't help myself.

The incident with the weed could have been a turning point for me. I started thinking how much I needed my independence. I needed my own place where I could do what I wanted. I started working towards what I thought was my freedom.

I told Mum shortly after this weed incident that I didn't want to go to college to do animation but instead wanted to work. I explained that later on maybe I would go to college, but for now I wanted to get out there and earn a living.

One of the agencies I'd reached out to after I finished school wanted to give me a job, but I needed to be 18 to work in a warehouse. I was thinking that as soon as I turned 18 and could get that job, I would move out and get my own place. I hadn't considered all the details of what that meant. All I was thinking about was that I would soon be able to do what I wanted without a parent looking over my shoulder.

15

Moving Out?

I soon realised there were a lot of holes in my plan to move out. My mum spent one evening giving me the details of what living on my own entailed: the costs involved and that the best I could hope for was a shared house (I would be living among strangers since I had no friends to share a house with). I was particular about my personal space and the utensils I used. If there was a speck of food on the dishes or cutlery after they had been washed in the dishwasher, I wouldn't use them. As one of my tasks was emptying the dishwasher every morning, I was familiar with bits of food getting stuck to the dishes and I would make a fuss if I had unknowingly put the cutlery in my food.

I was also a germaphobe; I wouldn't sit at the table with my brother at mealtimes if he had a cough or a cold. I didn't want to catch what he had. We were currently in a pandemic, and whilst my family got on my nerves, at least I felt safe that no one was going to bring coronavirus into our house. Mum was the "wash your hands" police!

I think I knew deep down that my family cared about me, but I felt so lost in my head that I couldn't see it. Maybe because I had been discussing moving out and Mum didn't want this to happen. When we extended our home from a three-bedroom to a four-bedroom, I got my own room, but I still had bunkbeds. Mum talked about redecorating, which included getting new furniture and buying me a double bed. I had asked a few times in the past when I would get one.

"When you start keeping your room tidy and stop throwing your clothes on the floor," Mum replied.

I gave it some thought for a minute and then dismissed the idea. It's not that I thought it was a bad idea, but I was fine with how my room was and wouldn't welcome any change.

Around this time, I was doing a lot of research on topics that would have given my parents a heart attack if they had known. I was also seeking advice from online acquaintances whom I felt comfortable with. I had concluded just after the summer of 2020 that there was only one way I could have my independence and be free of my constant loneliness and torment. I wasn't willing to share it with anyone who knew me except the people I knew online.

I had faith in God, but I had given up on praying and talking to God. In the past, Mum had encouraged me to pray and trust God with my problems, and sometimes I felt that my prayers had been answered. But I began questioning: If God was really listening to me, why was I feeling the way I was?

I was curious about what happened after death and tried to discuss this with my brother one day when we were out in the garden doing fitness training.

"What do you think about the afterlife?" I asked him. "Do you think there's life after death? What do you think happens when we die?"

"I don't know," he said. Then, after giving it some thought, he replied, "You should speak to Mum—and anyway, why are you asking?"

"No reason. Just curious."

Around this time there were huge debates going on about George Floyd's murder by the policeman in America, so I used this as an excuse to ask more about the details of what might have happened to him after his death.

I tried not to show too much interest in case my brother got suspicious. I didn't want anyone to know my thoughts and what my plans were. This was one of the reasons I did my research late at night after everyone else had gone to bed.

I could imagine how bad it would be if Mum found out after I'd said nothing was wrong and had refused professional help. I continued to research online, reading academic papers from Oxford and Cambridge on the whos, wheres, and whens on the topics I was interested in. I read about what had been done, and what was successful and what wasn't. In my family I was known for getting things wrong, so I wanted to make sure I got this right. On too many occasions I had rushed into things without giving them proper consideration, and then they backfired on me.

For example, I tried to order a bag for my paper round because the one I had was broken. I ended up ordering three different types of bags, even though Mum had told me to measure the current one and use the size for guidance. I got it wrong three times and had to return two bags. I had to keep the last one because I couldn't return it.

So I had to make sure I got this right. I'd read about those who got it wrong and had to face their family and the aftermath. I couldn't let that happen. I didn't want to live to tell the story afterwards.

I had several conversations with people who I regularly chatted with online. Some were shocked at some of the questions I was asking and encouraged me to speak to my parents or someone professional as I needed help. I was done with that. I had to take matters into my own hands to get the freedom I craved.

My 18th birthday was approaching, and Mum asked me what I wanted. I said I didn't want anything. What was the point? I didn't plan to be here much longer after my 18th birthday, although I had no date in mind. To me it was pointless making my usual list.

To compromise, I told Mum what I wanted to eat. I wasn't going to miss out on one of my favourite food of Chinese tapas. We were subject to very strict lockdown restrictions, so it would only be the four of us, which I was happy about. It had been almost a year of no family gatherings, and in a way I was thankful for that. I'm sure Mum would have wanted to invite family to celebrate my 18th birthday.

16

Is There Something about December?

I had no date or time in mind for when I would do it. I guess when it was the right time, I would know. That was what I told myself.

The night of Thursday, 10th December was like any other night. I had dinner and went up to my room as usual and continued to play Habbo on my laptop. Mum came into my room to tell me to take my laundry downstairs. Soon after she left, I was downstairs with my laundry. She was quite surprised to see me so soon because this wasn't usually the case. I smiled and didn't say anything.

Later I came downstairs and put a pizza in the oven, which I ate later. My brother loaded up the dishwasher and went upstairs to his bedroom. I was alone downstairs, eating the last of my pizza whilst I continued to play Habbo. Before I finished eating, my dad came in to give me some instructions on what I should do in the morning, as I needed to go to the bank and get verified in person so that I could get my Child Trust Fund. I was now 18, and the money would be transferred to my bank account.

As Dad spoke, I thought about the obstacles I had encountered with the form and with getting the money transferred to my account. Something I had thought would be simple had become a problem, with the bank of the Child Trust Fund asking for more information and verification. I thought about Thursday, a week ago, which was my birthday. I'd had my favourite food, and Mum surprised me with lager since I could now legally drink alcohol.

I remember sneakily drinking all four bottles of lager, even though I was only supposed to have one. I thought about the card that Mum and my brother had personally created with pictures of me and special words, and the gifts I had received that I wasn't expecting—two Nike hoodies—even though I had told her I didn't want anything. I thought about the cash gifts from friends and family who had dropped off cards or put money directly into my account. I had received more than one hundred pounds. Then I thought about the disappointment of being forced to buy joggers with some of the money, because Mum said I needed to have something tangible to look back on and not spend it all on McDonald's.

Little did she know I had no plans to be here. I had already taken a big step and ordered a rope the day after my birthday. I knew it was just a matter of time for me to end it.

I heard Dad say, "Did you hear what I said?" and that brought me back to the present and where I was.

"Yes," I responded, looking him in the eye. I wasn't going to tell him I only heard half of what he'd been telling me. In any case I could do it on Monday if I couldn't remember what I needed to do tomorrow. It would annoy him that he would have to repeat it all again, but it didn't matter.

He left me and went upstairs, and I was finally on my own. I finished my pizza, so I went upstairs to my bedroom with no intention of going back downstairs.

Whilst in my bedroom my thoughts went back to my life, as

usually happens every night. The call I had with an agency just two days ago came to mind. This was the same agency who had told me when I was looking for a summer job that I was guaranteed a warehouse job when I turned 18. I recalled how excited I was to call him and remind him that I was now 18. The anticipation shrivelled as the same issue cropped up again.

"Are you available for seven days a week? We want someone who is flexible to do any day in the week."

"Errm, I'm looking for part-time work." I had done the same thing as I did at the interview with McDonalds. I could not bear to do full time because of my social anxiety of being around strangers.

I could have kicked myself when he said, "Sorry, we only want someone who can do full-time."

I realised I had messed up again. Mum had told me to say I was available for full time and then afterwards negotiate for part-time hours.

I was frustrated with myself. How was I going to make it if I couldn't hold a simple conversation? I started ruminating over the situations that had gone wrong, all the things I had messed up. I looked up my searches on Google and then I thought, what was stopping me from making tonight the night that I put an end to it?

I had a small bottle of vodka in my room, which I'd bought the day after my birthday since I could now legally buy alcohol. I had the rope; everyone was in bed with no intention of getting up again tonight. Could I do this now? I wondered. What was stopping me?

All I saw in front of me was more of the same. I was already dreading socialising at Christmas (not that there would even be any additional people apart from my immediate family). I knew there was no way I could get out of eating Christmas dinner at the table with my family. My mum had already told me we would all be sitting down at the table for Christmas dinner, as we had done in the past, and this year wouldn't be an exception. We had already had several heated arguments about having Christmas dinner at the dining table. We hadn't sat altogether for months because I'd avoided it since March 2020.

The more I thought about it, the more convinced I was. I had to do it tonight.

I put on one of the hoodies I had got from my parents for my birthday. I got the reel of rope from where I had hidden it and cut a good length with scissors. I practised according to the pictures I had seen on the internet and felt ready.

I carefully went downstairs. I knew my brother usually went to sleep late even though he was already in bed. I was careful not to make any noise going down the stairs. I opened the back door and got the garden chairs I needed for height and leverage.

I got the rope and the vodka. I contemplated doing it in the garage, but I wasn't sure how strong the rods in the roof of the garage were. I put the key to the garage in my pocket because I couldn't be bothered to go back inside the house. I decided to end it by the tree that had a very sturdy branch that could support me.

I hadn't planned it to be this day or night. I hadn't planned it to be this early in the morning of the next day when in a few hours I would have been getting up to do my paper round.

But somehow I knew this was the right time, and I did it.

PART II

The Aftermath of an
Irreversible Action

Prologue

There is a pain in my chest, it is a gripping pain almost stopping me from breathing. I have heard of emotional pain feeling like physical pain but never experienced it to this degree. I am feeling suffocated. It's like a ton of weight on my chest that I cannot shift.

I have only experienced something similar once, and this was years ago when we thought we had lost Marley whilst visiting my cousin.

We had gone round by my cousin's house for a birthday celebration. We were all in the living room eating and chatting. Later some of our party moved to the front garden of the house whilst some of us stayed in the living room. I had stayed in the living room when a few minutes later I noticed that Marley was not in the same room as me. I assumed that he was with my auntie in the front garden, but I did not feel right with just assuming, so I got up to check that he was there.

When I got to the front of the house where my cousin and the others were, there was no sign of Marley and they thought he was with me in the living room.

We started searching the house and soon realised he was nowhere in the house, not upstairs or downstairs. My heart was pounding, a fear that I have never experienced was creeping up on me, but I tried not to give in to my horrible imaginations. A toddler cannot disappear in a house. Where could a 2-year-old have gone with four adults in the house? These were some of the questions going through my head.

We started looking for him on the road outside the house and as we crossed the road, we saw him with a group of neighbors who said that they saw him crossing the road by himself and were wondering why he was by himself and trying to ask him who he was. Of course, he was only a toddler and was still learning to speak so they could not make sense of what he was saying. It was such a relief to find him and to hold him.

I could not begin to imagine all the things that could have gone wrong. He could have been run over by a car whilst he was crossing the road by himself, or someone could have snatched him.

I shudder with fear just thinking about it. I was so grateful to God for protecting him and keeping him safe from harm. That was then and for years after this incidence I made sure that he was always within my sight. For some years afterwards I was very overprotective of him as I did not want to go through those few minutes of not knowing where he was which had felt like hours.

Fast forward sixteen years later and I am here again with this feeling of a ton of weight on my chest, experiencing what I can only imagine feels like several knives being stabbed into my heart. The pain and agony of what I had felt all those years ago when Marley was a toddler could not be compared to what I was feeling now. It was far, far worse than anything I had felt or imagined.

1

Family Life

I was happy. We were a family of four: my husband and two sons. We weren't perfect, but we loved each other, and I made sure that we looked out for each other.

I had a really good career—in fact, I'd say I was almost at the peak of my career. I had never expected, when I came to the UK from Sierra Leone all those years ago, that I would be in an executive position not just looking after the UK and Ireland but also responsible for the rest of Europe.

We had a lovely home with plenty of space, after extending it six years ago, and a spacious garden where we had hosted many barbecues with family and friends.

We didn't have any health issues that weren't under control. I would say we were all in relatively good health; nothing to really cause alarm. I felt we were all in a good place as long as we stayed away from the virus that was taking over the world.

We hadn't long come back from a much-needed holiday in Sierra Leone, the country of my birth. I had reunited with family and friends I hadn't seen for quite a long time.

We had arrived in Sierra Leone on the night of Boxing Day (the day after Christmas), which was on a Thursday, so we could attend my niece's wedding that Saturday. It was a big event, and my husband and sons had never experienced an African wedding. I was really glad they could experience a really traditional celebration—with all the modern elements too, of course.

The traditional music and food on the day before the wedding, known as the bachelor's eve in the Krio culture, the costumes we all had to put on immediately after the church ceremony, the food, and the traditional dancing all contributed to make the holiday very special and gave my family an experience they would remember for years to come.

We also visited one of the natural beaches in the Peninsular and tasted the local cuisine at the houses of different family members and in restaurants. The hot weather of upper twenties and lower thirties centigrade also made the holiday special. Usually at this time of the year in England we would all be wrapped up in winter coats, scarves, and gloves, whilst here in Freetown we were enjoying lovely sunshine, sea, and sand.

The afternoon we left to fly back to England was bittersweet. I said goodbye to family members who were in their late 80s, and I wondered whether this was the last time I would see them on this side of eternity. I gave hugs and kisses with tears in my eyes as I tried to capture the feel and smell of my aunties who had watched me grow up from a baby and now embraced me as a mature woman, wife, and mother of two almost adult children.

And whilst I was concerned that I might not see my aging aunties again, it never crossed my mind that this would be the last time we would go on a holiday as a family of four and that it would be the last time family members in Sierra Leone would see all of us together.

As soon as we got back home, I told my family it was the last time we would all go on holiday together. Well, truer words had never been said! I was thinking about all the stress I'd had trying to get all the necessary vaccinations, visas, and other documentation needed for our travel. Added to this, one family member resisted the pending trip with no valid reason other than what I thought was the social anxiety that he usually experienced when in a crowd.

I had to persevere with every step of the arrangements with Marley telling me he wasn't going. To accommodate him, I booked a hotel, made sure we spent Christmas in England, and only planned the trip to last seven days to ensure that I didn't push him too much out of his comfort zone.

I'm quite sure that anyone would understand why the first thing I said when we were safely back in our house was that I wasn't doing it again!

My sons were fine with my outburst. I expect they were thinking, *Who wants to go on holiday with parents when we're aged seventeen and twenty?* Definitely young men who wanted to hang out with their own age group and do their own thing. I could tell from their expressions that's what they were thinking.

I slowly got over the stress of the trip and got back into the routine of work and home life. My older son's twenty-first birthday was approaching, and I was having concerns regarding Marley as he had still not agreed to retake his GSCEs. I knew it was already too late for him to take them in May or June because he wasn't prepared.

After putting it off for a while, I had a chat with Marley, and he told me he didn't want to go to college and instead preferred to get a job. In the meantime, he wanted me to give him some time to complete the animation video he had started creating before we went on holiday. I agreed to this, and life went on.

2

Can We Celebrate, Please?

It was already a month after we arrived back in England and the Covid-19 virus was slowly spreading to different countries, dominating the national news. I wasn't giving it too much attention as I thought that China was very far away, and I had a significant milestone to prepare for. The twenty-first birthday of my elder son was approaching, and I was determined to celebrate the day. I asked him what he wanted to do, and he said, "Nothing, really. Maybe order a takeaway?" which didn't sit well with me—significant birthdays should be celebrated.

"Don't you want me to book dinner for the four of us at a restaurant? It's not every day you get to be twenty-first!"

He agreed to dinner but was reluctant to have a family gathering; he didn't want any fuss. I told him I would keep it small and only invite immediate family. I was excited. I would soon be the mother of a twenty-one-year-old. I started planning; reaching out to immediate family to check availability, planning the menu and digging out photos and videos of infancy. Whilst doing this research I discovered photos and videos of Marley which I had forgotten about.

As the day approached, I realised I was the only one who was excited about the forthcoming celebrations. I didn't realise Marley had no clue about what was happening, because when we' discussed the details, he was in his room and wasn't part of the discussion. He wasn't happy when he found out that he was the last one to know.

I'm glad I pushed through with these plans though. It turned out that this was the last occasion for some of the family to see all of us as a family of four.

The day of his brother's birthday was very difficult; Marley was in a nasty mood. He didn't want to go for dinner and refused to wish his brother a happy birthday. I thought, *What's going on now?*

I was convinced that this wasn't normal behaviour and made up my mind to get Marley some help the following week, after the birthday celebrations were out of the way. I remember the dinner we had on that Thursday. It was a strange affair. Marley wouldn't interact with us even though he was sitting at the table. He had reluctantly wished his brother Happy Birthday during the journey to the restaurant since I had insisted. His body language spoke volumes; he would rather be anywhere than at dinner with us. He was only there because I wouldn't allow it to be any other way.

The Saturday family gathering was the same. As family members arrived—a total of ten people—he was reluctant to leave his room and greet them. I had to get him downstairs on two occasions to say hello.

Later, he was unhappy and ruminated about feeling awkward when he interacted with family members. I was quite concerned. He had hardly exchanged two words with his cousin, whom he usually got on with very well, during the whole time she was with us. And she had stayed overnight.

The following week I spoke to our private healthcare provider to confirm whether our cover included mental-health care. I was really happy when they said we were covered and thanked God for the company I work at who made this possible. I immediately gave them a summary of what the issues were and asked if someone from the mental-health team could assess him. Assessing him wasn't a problem; getting Marley to cooperate was the challenge!

I wasn't going to give up as I had done before. I knew I could entice him with his favourite food. I told him he had to take the call so he could be assessed as it was very obvious to me that something wasn't right. It was not normal that all he wanted to do was sleep and surfaced only to eat or do his paper round.

He took the call and was later diagnosed with mild depression. He was prescribed ten sessions with a therapist but only attended one. He kept telling me nothing was wrong with him, and he didn't need therapy.

As a mother you are torn between pushing or holding off. Were these just symptoms of normal teenage hormonal behaviour that he would grow out of, or was this something more? These are the sort of questions I was battling.

He had only attended the first therapy session before the UK was locked down because of coronavirus. Later, I found out from the therapist that he didn't disclose anything that would have indicated his suicidal thoughts. He had mentioned his social anxiety but nothing more, so there was no way he could have been diagnosed with something more serious than just mild depression. Since we were in lockdown after the first session, he couldn't continue with the therapy. It was put on hold until he could physically meet with the therapist again.

I had to think of ways to keep him out of his room. I came up with another solution to get him out of his room. He loved pizza and junk food, so I promised him more of these in the weekly shopping if he would do daily training sessions with his brother in the garden. For me it was more about getting him outside away from his numerous screens—TV, tablet, laptop, and mobile phone—and getting some exercise as I had read somewhere that this was good for depression.

This solution was fraught with arguments and disagreements between the two brothers. Since the only exercise Marley did was ride his bike for his paper round, he found it difficult to keep up with the training sessions his brother had put together for him. I had to intervene quite often because Marley was complaining it was too hard and he couldn't do it, but he still wanted the extra treats I had promised him. I asked his brother to go easy on him, make it lighter to start off with until he got used to it. All through the summer they persevered until it got to the point where his brother's patience ran out.

I decided to try something different. Since he was still refusing to continue with the therapy sessions, even though some of the lockdown restrictions had been lifted, I told Marley to do his own exercise, as long as he recorded it and shared it in our WhatsApp family chat group. Then he would get the additional pizzas and junk food he wanted.

He seemed happy with this, and I thought at least he would continue to release endorphins, which I understood triggered a positive feeling in the body. I thought this would be good for him and would improve how he felt about himself, which, in turn, might help shift the mild depression he had been diagnosed with.

I had no clue there were deeper and more alarming issues than those that had been diagnosed.

3

Never Saw This Coming

We were now into autumn, and I was seeing a difference in Marley. He wasn't as defensive and was more receptive to being corrected. I was pleasantly surprised when one evening he agreed to watch a movie downstairs with his brother. I remember being in bed and saying to his dad, "What a change in Marley." I never thought I would see the day when he would sit in the front room and watch a movie with his brother as he had become such a hermit, always in his room.

I was really pleased, and the next day I asked his brother, "How was your movie night with Marley?"

He responded that it had been a bit weird as Marley wouldn't stop talking. He had talked so much that afterwards he said his jaw was hurting. I found it strange that he had talked right through the movie but thought that maybe he was making up for all the time he hadn't interacted with us.

I continued to see small changes in him, and I was happy that he wasn't always running off to his room after mealtimes. I really thought things were changing for the better. I assumed the daily exercise was having an impact on his well-being.

I asked him what he wanted for his 18th birthday, which was a few weeks away. I wanted to be prepared. There was no plan to book a table for dinner because of coronavirus, so whatever we did would have to involve only the four of us and take place at home.

He declined any presents, even though I thought he would have jumped at the chance to get a new bike or something he needed. He conceded a little by telling me what he would like for dinner on his birthday. As with his brother, I refused to accept that he wanted nothing for his birthday and decided to get him something he had asked for during the summer. When I had got him some T-shirts in the summer, he also asked for Nike hoodies, so I ordered him two nice ones. I created a personalised birthday card for him online.

I was late ordering the birthday items and wasn't sure they would arrive in time. Fortunately, the hoodies and the card arrived on the day of his birthday, so we were able to give him the gifts and card. He wasn't overjoyed—that was his usual demeanour over the last two years—but at least he said thank you. I was a bit disappointed. I thought he would have been impressed with the personalised card. Later I found out that he'd told his brother he really liked it, even though he hadn't told me. Though we could not have family over, I made a video call to his auntie so she could see him and wish him happy birthday. There were also lots of calls from family and friends far and near.

With everything that had been going on, you would expect that I would have seen what was coming, but I didn't. None of us did. We were completely blindsided with no warning.

I shared with Marley that he would be getting his Child Trust Fund, which the government had started when he was born, and now that he was 18, the money would be transferred to his bank account. It would be his to spend however he wanted. I really thought he would be excited, but he seemed to just take in his stride with no outward emotion.

On a cold, cloudless December morning, I experienced the most traumatic event of my life.

I woke up quite early, as usual, to have a quiet time of prayer and reading my Bible and a devotional. I read the verse of the day and then went on to read about a woman named Martha who was in a refugee camp and had experienced the traumatic loss of her family; rebels had broken into her home and killed her husband and two of her sons whilst she and her 6-month-old son hid. I couldn't begin to imagine the pain and agony she must have gone through and silently asked, "God, how could you have allowed this to happen?"

Little did I know that Martha's story was preparing me for what I would be facing in a little under two hours. I was also astounded by Martha's faith and joy, which the author of the devotional wanted to bring to light. Despite the tragic loss of her family, she was full of joy, supporting the other refugees in the camp and ministering to them.

I finished my quiet time and proceeded to get ready for work. It was a Friday, the end of my work week. I was looking forward to some downtime, but of course I had to get through Friday first.

As I prepared for working from home, I went downstairs to boot up my laptop, turn off the outside light, and open the curtains. I was surprised that the light was still on, as this indicated that Marley hadn't left for his paper round. I checked the back door as is my usual routine but didn't realise the door wasn't locked until I came back downstairs the second time. I took out the washing from the washing machine with the intention of taking the bedsheets to hang outside when I came back downstairs.

Second time round, I noticed the back door leading to the garden wasn't locked with the key and assumed my younger son had left it unlocked after leaving for his paper round early in the morning. I thought he had got up when I went back upstairs.

I went back upstairs again and finished off getting ready whilst informing my husband that the back door was unlocked and our youngest must have left it open in his rush not to be late for his paper round.

I was back downstairs for the third time, and since it was cloudy and cold, I thought I would only hang out the bedsheet and put the rest of the clothing on the clothes airer.

I grabbed the navy-blue sheet, opened the door leading to the garden from the utility room, and saw something that no mother ever wants to see. *Am I awake?* I asked myself. *Am I really seeing what I'm seeing? Is it my imagination or is the sight in front of me for real? I must be in a trance because this can't be real. It's not true; it must be a mirage.*

In those few seconds, which felt like hours, I refused to accept that what I was seeing was reality. I felt I must still be asleep and having a nightmare.

I was in shock. I couldn't move for those few seconds, and then I shouted, "Marley, Marley!"

The sound of my voice didn't even seem like mine. I ran towards the mirage that unfortunately was reality.

From afar I had wondered who was standing under the tree in the garden. The person looked like Marley but appeared to be too tall. The clothes and trainers were Marley's, but with his back facing me, I couldn't tell whether it was really him. My head was also telling me that Marley had gone to do his paper round, so I couldn't work out why he would be standing under the tree.

God in his faithfulness knew I couldn't take the magnitude of the traumatic incident unfolding in front of me in one go, so it came to me in bits. When I got closer, I realised Marley was hanging with a rope round his neck tied to the tree. My immediate reaction was to try to get him off the tree, but I couldn't, so I had to rush into the house screaming for his dad and his brother as they were still in bed.

They rushed downstairs. They couldn't make sense of what I was saying, because I was crying and talking at the same time. I was shaking, but I managed to give them instructions to get him off the tree and bring him into the house. I really thought he had just passed out and could be revived. I was praying to God for miracles, I couldn't believe my baby boy was gone. In between the crying, I had managed to call the emergency services and the paramedics were on their way.

Meanwhile, before the paramedics arrived, I felt that I had to pray to God to bring him back. *He's only eighteen,* I thought, *and only last week we celebrated his birthday and told him what he could do now that he was legally considered an adult.*

I threw myself on him as his dad and brother laid him on the floor of the utility room.

"Jesus," I prayed, "you are the healer. You brought Lazarus back from the dead after three days, I'm trusting you now to bring Marley back. How could you take him? He has all his life ahead of him."

The paramedics arrived and asked us to go into the other room. They closed the door, and the three of us looked at each other in disbelief and despair. His brother was in tears, pacing the floor. I was crying and asking God *why?* I wasn't sure whether I was awake or still sleeping, and my husband was trying to be strong for all three of us.

It felt like an hour, but it was only ten minutes or so before one of the paramedics opened the door and told us that unfortunately, Marley was gone, and there was nothing more they could do.

I heard this wailing and didn't even recognise it was me until his brother put his arms around me to comfort me. I was devastated. I kept thinking I must still be asleep as it wasn't even half past nine yet. This couldn't be real.

4

Breaking the News

It was the evening of that traumatic day. The minutes and hours had flown by without me realising that the day was almost gone. I had made calls to family members and close friends shortly after we had the confirmation of death. The calls were really difficult to make. No one expected such devastating news.

The police later flooded the house to rule out any suspicious activity. They did forensics in his room, asked us questions, and took pictures of the tree and the immediate surroundings. We had discovered that he had the key to the garage in his pocket. A small, empty vodka bottle lay on the grass underneath the tree. The garden chairs were stacked together, with one chair directly underneath where I had found him hanging.

I had lots of questions without answers.

Slowly, we started piecing things together. The police had unlocked his phone, and in his Google searches, we saw that he had been researching ways to end his life. In his notepad he had also reflected on what would happen when someone ends his life and no longer had a physical body to do the things they used to do. We were shocked and unable to believe that our Marley, the youngest in the family, who wasn't streetwise and always needed a guiding hand, could have orchestrated this fatal act right underneath our noses without us having the slightest inkling of what he was planning.

In the midst of my despair, I recalled the devotional I had read in my quiet time that morning, the story about Martha, who had witnessed the murder of her husband and two sons whilst hiding from the rebels who had invaded her home. I really felt comforted. God has a way of speaking to us and preparing us for things to come. The story of Martha was God's way of preparing me for what I would go through when I discovered what Marley had done.

By now it was late in the evening, and I realised none of us had eaten or drunk anything all day apart from a few hot drinks.

Close family had come round and had now gone, and I had to find the strength to prepare some food for us. Nothing heavy, as we weren't hungry, but I knew we had to eat to keep our strength.

After we went through the motions of eating, there were still close family members who weren't aware of what had happened. I was conscious of how I shared this very sad and unexpected news. I called his godmother and asked her where she was as I didn't want to share the news if she was driving or in a public place. She knew everything about Marley; we had spent the last eighteen years praying and fasting for our children every first Saturday of the month.

She told me she was in the laundrette, so I asked her to call me when she was home, which turned out to be about an hour later. I knew how blindsided we were by discovering Marley this morning and tried to prepare everyone before I told them the horrible news. How do you share such devastating news with anyone who knew Marley as a quiet young man in good physical health with no noticeable illness?

It was hard. Everyone I told fell apart on the phone, totally devastated. In some cases, I was the one offering words of comfort. In other cases, it caused me to grieve all over again.

In the midst of my despair, there was also some anger. "How could Marley have thrown us into the spotlight when he hated the spotlight himself?" I asked myself.

I recalled questions upon questions from the police and the number of police cars outside the house. So many vehicles, in fact, that one of our neighbours had been texting me asking why. We had lived in this house for nearly seventeen years, and not once had we been the centre of attention. In their investigations, the police had to interview our immediate neighbours to ask if they had observed anything suspicious in the hours leading up to Marley's death.

Whilst I tried to prepare family and friends when I spoke to them before breaking the news about Marley, there were a few with whom I had been very blunt and direct in my narrative. One of these was my line manager. I was supposed to have joined an online meeting with her and another colleague, a regular meeting that we had every Friday. She had texted me and I was trying to text her back when she called me. I immediately started crying and just blurted out everything that had happened prior to her call.

At the time the house was still full of police, and I told her in gruesome detail what had happened and how I had found Marley. Later on, I would reflect back on that conversation and apologise to her for being so blunt, but at the same time I had to commend her for the way she handled such a critical moment. I will always remember her encouraging words in the midst of tears as she couldn't stop herself from being emotional after hearing such devastating news.

Another conversation during which I was brutally blunt was the call with the newsagent who employed Marley to do the paper round. We had seen a text message he had sent Marley when he hadn't turned up for his paper round that Friday morning. It wasn't a very encouraging message and it made me mad. I started thinking of all the times Marley had said he had been told he would lose his paper round if he was late again, and I knew how devastating that would have been for him.

Marley's phone was still unlocked and suddenly started ringing. It was a call from the newsagent. His brother didn't know whether he should answer so I took the phone from him and answered it.

The newsagent's first words were, "Where are you?"

As soon as I heard him, expecting to speak to Marley, asking where he was and not checking to see if he was OK, I just saw red and gave it to him straight. "Marley has killed himself."

He was stunned. I knew I had handled it badly, but I was high on emotion and wanted to lash out at someone, and he was the ideal candidate. At a later date, when he came round to properly sympathise, I shared some truths with him. I said that I considered him to be a kind of mentor to these young ones, as their first experience of earning money could be as a paperboy or papergirl. At that age they have no idea of the rules of earning a living. I told him he had an opportunity to mentor and coach and not be the hard taskmaster Marley had painted him to be in some instances.

Whether he took on board what I said I don't know, but I was glad I said my piece. I hope he did listen, for the sake of all the other young ones like Marley who depended on the paper round for that little bit of independence.

5

Surrounded by Love

I thought that the emotional roller coaster of the first day would be over in the coming days. I wasn't prepared for the firsts. The first time I came downstairs the next morning was tough. The night before, we had hardly slept. I lay in bed thinking about what had happened, swaying between a sort of reality and a dreamlike state, not sure if someone was going to wake me up and tell me it was a nightmare, that it didn't really happen, whilst all the images kept going round and round in my head. I couldn't get rid of them no matter how hard I tried. I would later realise it is hard to get rid of these images.

I couldn't stay in bed any longer after tossing and turning all night. I got up and went downstairs. It was about five thirty in the morning and I could hear Marley's alarm for his paper round going off on his phone, even though the phone was off. I went to his room and took the phone downstairs with me. Seeing that the outside light was still on got me emotional as Marley was always the first downstairs and he would turn off the light.

I started crying and praying at the same time. I was crying to God, asking where Marley was now. After bringing him up in church and taking him to Sunday school, I wanted assurance that he was with Jesus. I recalled all the conversations we'd about God and the prayers we had shared. I recalled him telling me once that it was like he had two voices speaking to him sometimes, and he knew it was the devil and Jesus, but he didn't listen to the devil.

I was down on my knees on the floor of the utility room where the day before I had been crying to God to raise him back to life. Now I was asking God to let me know that he had him. If Marley wasn't here with me, where I could continue to nurture him, I needed the assurance that he was in heaven.

Whilst I was praying silently and sobbing loudly, his brother came downstairs and gave me a hug. He said, "Marley is at peace. He is no longer troubled."

I immediately felt a calmness and assurance that I couldn't explain. I felt the peace according to what is written in the Bible: "And the peace of God [that peace which reassures the heart, that peace] which transcends all understanding, [that peace which] stands guard over your hearts and minds in Christ Jesus [is yours]" (Philippians 4:7 Amplified Bible)

Another first was unloading the dishwasher. I started and couldn't finish, as it was a stark reminder that Marley would never do this again. This was Marley's chore that he did every morning after his paper round. Even when he was still at school, he unloaded the dishwasher before going to school. On this occasion, his brother had to finish.

The cupboard and freezer were full of the food he loved, as our monthly shopping had only been delivered two days before his demise. Looking at all the food that only Marley loved, I burst into tears. I experienced what almost felt like physical stabs to my heart. I was sobbing and devastated all over again.

I turned to God. "How could you let this happen?" I asked in my despair. Never to see that cheeky smile again. Never to hear him talk to me and exchange opinions. It was hard; it was unbearable, but I had to hold on, and I could only do it with the help of God.

I have lost close family members: my dad, my mum, siblings, aunties, and cousins, but nothing prepared me for the pain and emptiness of losing a child. It definitely wasn't the normal order of how things should be. As parents, we're supposed to die before our children, not the other way round.

In the midst of my despair, I heard a voice say to me, "I would not let you be tempted more than you can handle. Of all the alternatives available, this was the one that you could bear, which is why I allowed it."

I started to think about what some of these alternatives could have been. Marley could have been unsuccessful in taking his life, but in the process he could have damaged his brain and never been the same again. Or we could have got there just after he lost consciousness and saved him, but then forever lived in fear of him doing it again as all trust would have been eroded.

This verse came to mind:

> No temptation [regardless of its source] has overtaken or enticed you that is not common to human experience [nor is any temptation unusual or beyond human resistance]; but God is faithful [to His word—He is compassionate and trustworthy], and He will not let you be tempted beyond your ability [to resist], but along with the temptation He [has in the past and is now and] will [always] provide the way out as well, so that you will be able to endure it [without yielding and will overcome temptation with joy]. (1 Corinthians 10:13 AMP)

The first time going into his room was tough. It was a mess, what with the untidy state Marley kept it in, plus all the debris the police had left after their investigation. A few days later I felt the urge to tidy it up. I pushed through the pain as I realised it needed to be done. His room wasn't going to be that part of the house we didn't dare visit. I tidied up a bit and threw away all the rubbish.

The next day after he was gone, was the first Saturday when we did the deep cleaning as a family, this was really difficult. None of us felt like it; it would be too hard. Who would clean the mirrors and do the dusting, not to mention the vacuuming, which was Marley's task? None of us fancied it. So, we did a little tidying and left it for another day.

We constantly got phone calls as the news spread from one family member or friend to the other. I couldn't tell everyone, so there were some family members given the task of telling others and, likewise, the same for friends. We spent that weekend trying to tell all our close friends and family members. Cards and flowers were being delivered in a steady stream from people far and wide.

The love we received was overwhelming, and we were thankful to know that people cared for us. But at the same time we were having to repeat some of the same answers over and over again to the same questions, as most people asked the same things: "Were there any signs?" "Did you know he was suicidal?" We found this quite overwhelming.

One of my friends asked me what I wanted from her and how she could support me. At the time I had no clue what I wanted or needed. I had never lost a child before. I didn't know what to say to her. She immediately said she would bring food the next day and later organised a rota for all the local friends who wanted to bring food. We didn't want two or three people delivering food on the same day.

In the months that followed she also organised a few friends to deliver something on the eleventh of each month to cheer me up. Sometimes it was flowers, sometimes a fruit basket, and sometimes something to pamper myself. Another close friend also decided she would bake a cake every two weeks and drop it off.

Our pastor was also very supportive. He turned up with a bagful of goodies, from facial tissues to a box of chocolates; cleaning stuff for the dishwasher, mousse for hair—it seemed everything was in that bag. He helped us get the gate fixed as well because, in the rush for the emergency services to get into our house on the day, the gate had been kicked down and was hanging by a nail. He was also supportive when we needed to go to the funeral home and make the arrangements.

These and many more tokens of love kept us going during the first few weeks. I remember another friend deciding to cook and serve soup in takeaway cups for us to have at the cemetery, since it was a cold day, and we couldn't have a repast because of the Covid restrictions.

Friends prayed with me every single day, and others prayed with me fortnightly, and of course I continued with my monthly fast and prayer. Other friends went for walks with me so that I got out of the house and had some fresh air. At the time it wasn't obvious to me how much I needed this until I got outside. I realised that only God could see me through this. If he wasn't going to stop it, then he already had a plan for me to get through it.

I was constantly playing or singing this song about God's goodness (written by Jason Ingram, Ed Cash, Brian Mark Johnson, Jenn Louise Johnson, and Ben David Fielding):

> From "Goodness of God"
> I love You, Lord.
>
> ...
>
> I love Your voice.
> You have led me through the fire
> In the darkest night.
> You are close like no other.
> I've known You as a Father.

I've known You as a Friend,
And I have lived in the goodness of God (yeah)

This song was my daily anthem. I needed to remind myself that all my life, God has been faithful; he hadn't suddenly abandoned me because I lost Marley. He is still the same God. He still loves me the same. I was also touched when I received a letter from a resident of one of the houses Marley delivered newspapers to during his paper round. This elderly man, who had the same name as my husband, had taken the time to share with us how Marley had helped him set up payments for his newspapers at the height of the lockdown, as he was shielding and couldn't go out to pay for them. Marley had never mentioned it, and I felt comforted that he was being helpful to others as we had taught him from a young age.

6

Staying Strong

The pain didn't decrease; the pain in my heart didn't lessen. I was constantly swaying from one emotion to another: Guilt for not realising Marley was going through much deeper mental anguish than I had thought, anger that he should have taken such an action without sharing his feelings with us, sadness because I felt he had taken a lonely journey while we were all asleep in bed, fear of losing anyone else in our family, and helpless because there was nothing I could do to bring him back.

Surprisingly, I felt I was drawing closer to God, for, as the bible says,

"The Lord is near to the heartbroken and He saves those who are crushed in spirit (contrite in heart, truly sorry for their sin)" (Psalm 34:18 AMP).

Marley's photos and videos, the ones we had taken over the

years, and especially when he was younger, were a source of comfort to me.

My husband asked me, "Why are you watching that? Doesn't it make you sad?"

I had said no, because if anything, it brought him back to life. We had captured a memory of a moment in time when he was laughing or talking or doing everyday stuff. When I yearned to hear his voice, I listened to some of the last WhatsApp voice messages he had sent me telling me something or asking me to get something from the supermarket on my way home.

I discovered in those early days that though we all loved Marley in our family, the relationship we shared with him was very different. The mother-son relationship was very strong, having carried him for more than nine months in the womb, I had always been his go-to person when he needed anything. It was usually the two of us in the morning trying to step out of each other's way as we prepared our breakfast when he got home from his paper round.

There was emptiness when I got downstairs first thing, and for weeks after his death I would be in tears, missing our special moments.

It was only the Monday of that same week that he had come back from his paper round with issues with his bike.

"I should have asked for a new bike when you asked me what I wanted for my birthday," he had said.

"Really, it's not too late. I could still get you a new bike."

"Nah."

Even though I had bought him Christmas gifts already, I would have got him the bike too as I usually liked to get gifts that are needed. Instead, he told his dad about his latest bike issues, as he usually fixed any issues that didn't need a bike specialist.

When I think of that week, a few things caused me to ponder. Marley asked me for things I would normally have refused because he already had them, but for some reason it was as if my spirit knew this was my last opportunity to say yes and that I would regret it later if I said no.

For example, he loved apple pies and already had a box of six from the shopping, which was delivered on the Tuesday before his death on the Friday. On the Wednesday, he asked if he could have some from the other box of six, and usually I would have said no and told him that there were other people in the house who hadn't yet had their share, but on this occasion I said yes. He also asked for some Pringles, which I gave him, and the remainder of the pack was later found in his room. He went on to ask me for my can of Coke, which I would generally have refused him, and for once I actually said yes. He was quite surprised at the time!

These were little things that I recalled later on, and it gave me peace that I had said yes when usually I would have said no.

As we huddled together in our grief on that fateful day, one of the first things we had to do was get the tree cut down. I made a call on the very day he passed to get the tree taken away, as it was one of the first things that we found difficult: going into the garden and seeing the tree brought it all back.

Two days later the tree was gone, and we could breathe a bit more freely. I sometimes wonder why he had the key to the garage in his pocket. He had no reason to have gone into the garage as he hadn't hidden the rope there. We later found the whole reel of rope in his room behind his chest of drawers. I concluded that he must have thought of doing it in the garage, but the rods holding the roof may not have looked strong enough. Since he wanted to ensure it was a successful action, he didn't want to take a chance.

I really thank God that it wasn't in the house or the garage as we would have found it difficult to stay here. As it is, because it was outside and on a tree, we could easily get rid of the tree whilst creating a flowerbox where the tree had been as a memory to Marley.

The Bible says, "In every situation [no matter what the circumstances] be thankful and continually give thanks to God;

for this is the will of God for you in Christ Jesus" (1 Thessalonians 5:18 AMP).

There are several interpretations to this verse, but I always look at it this way: we should always be thankful because we're created to be grateful. It's God's will for us to be thankful. Whatever the situation, there is usually a worse position that you could be in than whatever your circumstances are.

Some may disagree with me, but I can't imagine the emotions of other mums like Martha (in my devotional) or countless other women who have lost their sons due to someone taking their lives. For me, though, that wasn't how it happened, and Marley wasn't killed by someone else. Though he wasn't in a good mental state when he made the decision to end his life, no one took his life away from him.

7

Difficult Days

How we got through the pain of Christmas Day without Marley, God only knows. We tried doing something different from what we would normally do and ate Christmas dinner in front of the television instead of at the dinner table. There was no way we could handle sitting at the dining table as it would have been unbearable to have three place settings instead of the usual four, with one significant person missing at the table. It was bearable doing something different.

I gave Marley's Christmas gifts to friends of his who would appreciate them, as I didn't want to see them in the house after the person they were intended for was no longer with us.

After Christmas Day we had to prepare for the viewing at the funeral home and then the service itself. I was so thankful that we could have the burial before the New Year. We had agreed with our pastor and the funeral home that we would have the service on Tuesday, 29 December 2020.

Planning the service, putting together the order of service, and working out who, out of the numerous family members and friends, would attend in person, along with those who had played a part in Marley's young life and who wanted to have the opportunity to do something in the service, was a challenge. We made it work, especially writing the eulogy. It was definitely a family affair put together by the three of us and his cousin, who read the eulogy.

As a family we grew stronger, because, with strict lockdown at the time, we couldn't have anyone from outside our household visiting. All food deliveries had to be made at the door. We had to be dependent on each other with regular check-ins on how we were feeling. As an individual I grew stronger as I learned to lean more on God than anyone else.

I still had lots of questions and over the course of time I started getting answers. Some of those answers came from unexpected sources. I spoke to a close confidante on Christmas Day, and she told me about a friend who was moving to another country because her son had tried to take his life and was now sectioned, so she couldn't bear to stay in England anymore. I reflected on that, and I realised that I would have found it really hard to bear if Marley had ended up in a similar situation.

When I kept thinking about why he had done it and where his head was at the time, I had a dream in which Marley said to me "I'm sorry, I'm sorry, I was having dark, dark thoughts." I felt comforted because in the dream his voice was so clear to me, and it was almost as if I was awake.

In early January about a month after his demise, I discovered that he had been researching this for a long time and conversing with different people online. I also found out what day he had ordered the rope and why we had no inkling as usually either my husband or I will be the ones to receive any delivery. He had the foresight to get it delivered to a collection point and not to our house. He was determined not to be found out. I imagined the fallout if we had found out before he did it. How would he have felt and how would we have felt? I concluded that it would have been terrible, as all trust would have been gone.

A week after Marley passed, I got the strong impression that I needed to do something with my pain. A few people had asked how I wanted to remember Marley, and I couldn't think clearly then. But later it became clear to me from this scripture, which was one of the readings at the service for Marley.

The Bible says, "I assure you and most solemnly say to you, unless a grain of wheat falls into the earth and dies, it remains alone [just one grain, never more]. But if it dies it produces much more grain and yields a harvest. John 12:24 AMP).

I felt this compelling need to help other children who are experiencing the same or similar mental illness as Marley.

If this traumatic incident hadn't happened, I would never have thought of that. Since it had, I had an opportunity to turn my pain into something beneficial for others. The idea to combine what Marley loved to do and the struggle he had with anxiety and depression gave birth to Marley's Aart Foundation (https://www. marleysaartfoundation.com/). Somehow, I had to use art to help those with similar mental health issues.

Soon after, I got confirmation from a close family friend whilst she was praying with me. Her daughter had a dream, and in the dream Marley was all dressed up, looking relaxed, teaching, and supporting children with art. I shared with her the inspiration I'd recently had, and we both said this was confirmation.

8

Hope amid Pain

The day of Marley's burial was very difficult, but surprisingly it got better as the day unfolded. The night before the service—and I say service because I still can't say the word funeral—I remember thinking, *How will I get through tomorrow?*

I knew the itinerary by heart—what time the hearse would leave the funeral home, what time it would arrive at our house, and the route it would take to the church. I had given the funeral home the route as this was the way we had gone so many times before. I was wondering if I would be able to compose myself; waves of uncontrollable loss rolled over me from moment to moment.

The Bible says, "'Listen to Me,' [says the Lord], 'O house of Jacob, and all the remnant of the house of Israel, You who have been carried by me from your birth and have been carried [in my arms] from the womb, even to your old age I am He, and even to your advanced old age I will carry you! I have made you and I will carry you; be assured I will carry, and I will save you'" (Isaiah 46:3–4 AMP).

These verses really spoke to me and reminded me that God was with me and would continue to be with me.

When I needed something to hold on to, God in his amazing love reminded me about something I had experienced earlier in 2020 when I was travelling back to England on my way home from a business trip. I had looked out the window of the plane and saw a plane in the clouds surrounded by what looked like a rainbow or a ring of fire, travelling parallel to us. After a few seconds of watching this image in awe and wonder, I took my phone and recorded it. I wanted to capture this amazing image.

As I continued to watch, it dawned on me that the plane I could see was the plane I was on—the sun had projected the image that I was seeing on the clouds. I was amazed at the awesomeness of God. The ring of rainbow or fire was telling me that God is in control, that he was the one carrying us in this plane.

I have travelled a lot for business and for pleasure, but the incredible achievement of a plane being in the air never gets old for me. Whilst there is a lot I do not understand about the physics of it all, there is one thing I know for sure: God gave human beings the brains and know-how to do and create such amazing things. I didn't know how much this would come to mean to me later in the year, but at that time I felt this assurance that God's got me, and he wanted to show me in a physical way by allowing me to see this through the window.

As I reflected on this, I felt that the same God would be with me through the difficult day in front of me and the days ahead. I thought about how it feels for a parent to bury a child, as it is not the normal order of how things should be. And I thought about burying my own son, for whom I had so many hopes and dreams and ambitions, and I broke down in tears.

The hours leading up to the arrival of the hearse at our house were torture. I had felt the emotions bubbling underneath the surface, and my hands shook as I put on my white dress. We had agreed that the colour for all the women attending the service would be white, representing innocence.

It was an effort to get ready. I kept looking out the window, thinking about the number of times in the past when I would get ready for work and look out this very window. I would see Marley's friend, who later moved north, waiting for him so they could ride to school together. Later on, after he left school, I looked out the window and saw him coming home from his paper round. And now I couldn't believe I would never see him on his bike again.

When I heard the doorbell ring, I knew the hearse was outside. I couldn't stop myself from breaking down into uncontrollable tears. I heard the funeral director speaking to me and the words, "Sorry for your loss," but the rest of it was just noise in the background as I looked at the hearse and tried to comprehend that Marley, my Marley, was in that vehicle.

Because of strict lockdown restrictions we couldn't have a car for the family, but my friend had volunteered to be our chauffeur for the day, and somehow she managed to lead me to her car. We all got in and were on our way. I was sitting in the back with Marley's brother, and through my tears I saw some of my neighbours outside and along the road adjacent to our house. I also saw a couple from our church who lived quite close to us standing by the roadside paying their respects.

I was crying uncontrollably, and even the song that was my anthem ("Goodness of God," sung by Tasha Cobbs Leonard) couldn't stop the tears from flowing down my face.

When we got to the church, some of my friends from the Ladies Bible Study group stood opposite the church as we walked in. I was really touched, and this really comforted me. Indeed, God was carrying me through this. Though I couldn't physically see him, the love and commitment from the ladies, standing outside for the seventy-five-minute service because they couldn't go inside due to Covid restrictions, said a thousand words. I was grateful, and as the service commenced, I got stronger and focused on celebrating Marley's shorter-than-expected life.

After the burial we lingered for a while at the cemetery, a time of reflection and refreshments for those who had attended the funeral, since there couldn't be a repast or reception indoors. Through the foresight of a friend, we had soup served in takeaway cups to keep us warm. I had some time to show gratitude to all who had attended, including a few family members and friends who had travelled from Oxford, London, Reading, Kent, and Northampton, all of us united in our grief, each trying to make sense of it all.

Later when we arrived home, there were mixed emotions. On one hand this terrible day was almost over, but with it was also the finality of burial. Our close friends from Reading had followed us home as I had brought over some gifts from friends in Sierra Leone earlier in the year that they needed to collect. In a way it was good that we had this diversion because if we hadn't, we would have been on our own soon after we were dropped off. Whilst they couldn't enter the house, we chatted with them outside and felt comforted by their presence.

Later I spoke to my brother in Sierra Leone and was touched when he told me that even in the pandemic, about fifty people consisting of family and close friends had attended the service they had at their house directly after streaming the service for Marley on YouTube. I was told it was emotional and there were tears over there as cousins and aunties also paid tribute to Marley. On YouTube, I later saw all the messages that had been left by friends and family from all over the world.

Again, as before, I was touched how God had used so many people to show me love and comfort during a difficult period. With the time difference in America, I was amazed that even friends and family from that side of the ocean had joined the live service.

9

Being Comforted

As a family, we're still navigating the aftermath of losing Marley, but we're moving forward with Marley in our hearts. There are difficult days ahead, such as the opening of the inquest and the actual inquest hearing. I had already spoken several times to the coroner's officer. A death such as suicide would always be reported to the coroner. The coroner's officer, on behalf of the coroner, will try to gain a better understanding of what happened to the person who took his own life. They gather evidence and information to help understand the circumstances leading to that suicide. They are required to start the process as soon as possible, and this is known as opening an inquest. This is usually a brief meeting in the coroner's court, allowing them to adjourn (postpone) the full inquest to a later date to allow sufficient time for information to be gathered. I hope I will be feeling stronger when we have to attend the inquest.

The Bible says, "When you pass through the waters, I will be with you; and through the rivers, they will not overwhelm you. When you walk through the fire, you will not be scorched, nor will the flame burn you" (Isaiah 43:2AMP).

God promises to be with us in all these different situations. We feel the waters as we go through the river, feel the splashing of the water, feel the force of it trying to pull us under—just as the traumatic event of Marley's suicide tried to pull us down into grief—but we weren't in any way submerged by it because every step of the way, God was letting us know he was there. The image of what we saw in the garden on that fateful day was imprinted in our memories and may be for a very long time. In those early days we couldn't shake it from our thoughts, and from moment to moment we felt the heat of it, but we weren't burned even though there were times when it felt like it.

God cares, and we're reminded of this on a daily basis. Our pastor reminded us in his message on the day of the service; we don't have the answers to all the questions we have regarding Marley's death, but God still cares.

The support of our church family and our friends and relations has been tremendous. The individual professional counselling we had in the first ten weeks after the burial helped us open up and talk about Marley. We're constantly reminiscing about what he would think or do in different situations we have experienced without him.

For instance, when it was his brother's 22nd birthday, we decided we would have a McDonald's meal in honour of Marley. I ordered a Big Mac for myself as this was Marley's favourite.

When I introduced a new meal into our dinnertime, I said to his brother, "Guess who would have loved this meal?"

He immediately said Marley because it included a burger and fries.

When I received a Google Nest home automation system as a Christmas gift from work, we all immediately said that Marley would have taken great pleasure in saying, "Hey, Google, can you tell me this or that?" He was very opinionated and always liked to have the last word and would have loved to prove he was right by asking Google Nest. We're constantly bringing his name into our conversations to keep his memory alive.

When his brother tripped in the garden because it was slippery, he couldn't help but think that Marley would have laughed his head off if he could have seen him, and maybe he did see him because he was there in spirit. Only God knows.

When I reached out for a tissue from the box and realised there were none because someone had taken the last one, I had to say, "Sorry, Marley. I thought you were the only one who left the tissue box empty after taking the last one, but now I know it wasn't only you."

Whilst we move forward and take him with us, we know that family celebrations and events will never be the same, and for me, the eleventh as a date will always bring back memories of Marley. When the date and the day of the week coincide, it will always be harder, but knowing that there is a legacy that will help others will continue to give me hope and spur me on.

Amongst all the love and support we were shown daily, I was pleasantly surprised when my manager from my previous employers told me she had written a song about Marley. She felt inspired after watching the service on YouTube for a second time and felt that the words of the song were given to her. God indeed works and moves in mysterious ways.

10

Be Encouraged

I'm a Christian and have a very strong faith in God. Not everyone will understand the Bible references in the latter chapters, but I included the references and the gospel song for those who will understand the context and draw strength from them. I'm aware that there will be a lot of people from other faiths or religions who will read this book, and I would like to say I can only refer to what I know and what has really been my source of strength during this difficult time. There are also others who have no faith or religion, and I hope you are also able to get something out of reading this book.

I would like to encourage any parent who has children who are showing similar symptoms to Marley's to follow your gut feeling. Sometimes as parents we can only do what we can with the knowledge we have, so don't beat yourself up if you don't always get it right. Being a parent is something none of us received formal training for. In some cases, we may have been fortunate enough to have parents or older family members or friends who guided us when we were faced with situations we hadn't navigated before.

Whilst there are books on parenting that can guide us, reading the concepts and experiencing the reality can be two completely different things. We have to trust God if we believe in him, and if we don't, we must trust our instincts that we're doing the right things for our children.

It's also important to keep in mind that not all children who show the same symptoms as Marley will take an action that ends with an irreversible and a traumatic situation. Some may just be experiencing preteen or teenage hormones. Parents, do all you can to get younger children showing similar symptoms diagnosed to rule out any early stages of mental-health issues, since they are more receptive to intervention at an early age and are less likely to be stigmatised by what their peers might say.

They might fight you all the way but trust your parental instincts that you are doing the right thing. At the end of the day, you want to do all you can for your child, and whilst he or she might not understand all the whys and wherefores, you want that assurance that you did all you possibly could.

For those parents who have gone through a similar traumatic experience, I hope that what I have shared encourages you. There are many questions I still don't have answers for, but I know God is with me. Don't for one minute believe that something you did or didn't do led to your traumatic event. Don't think that God has left you or forsaken you because if you looked closely, you would realise he is the one behind the unexpected phone call or the card with encouraging words. He prompted the person who called you when you were feeling your lowest.

As I thought about what could have been going on in Marley's mind, I was questioning: Did he care for me, for his dad and his brother? Why would he put us through this trauma? I beat myself up as to how I could have missed the signs. If I don't know what signs to look for how could I know when I had missed it. These were some of the thoughts I had, and God sent friends of mine who are experienced mental-health practitioners to give me insight. Through their expertise, I clearly understand that when a person gets to the point when he decides to end his life, he's not thinking of how devastated his loved ones will feel or what the consequences of his actions will be.

For any young adults going through what Marley went through, I encourage you to seek help. There are lots of successes with therapy, and suicide is not a solution. Though you may feel like you're alone, there are many others having similar anxious thoughts. Reach out to organisations that can help you and be willing to put the coping mechanisms that they provide into practice. Also, don't reach out to people you consider online friends who really don't have the answers and probably don't even know you very well. Find someone you can trust and speak to them. A family member who you feel close to, or a family friend would be a good place to start. Don't take an action that will be permanent with no do-over. It's definitely not the answer.

"Marley's Song" by M. Grant
No, this is not goodbye;
It's just the start of something new.
I'll be right by your side
And hold your hand to help you through.
I'll shine a light to show you
I haven't gone away,
And I will glow within your heart
For ever and a day.
No, this is not goodbye;
It is just the start of something new.

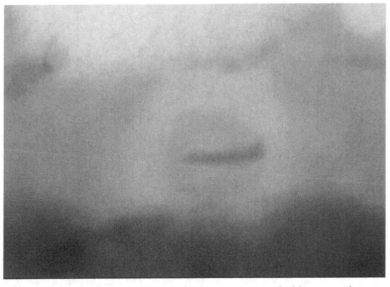

Image of the plane I was travelling in surrounded by a rainbow.

Printed and bound by CPI Group (UK) Ltd, Croydon, CR0 4YY